Generations, culture and society

Generations, culture and society

JUNE EDMUNDS AND
BRYAN S. TURNER

OPEN UNIVERSITY PRESS
Buckingham · Philadelphia

Open University Press
Celtic Court
22 Ballmoor
Buckingham
MK18 1XW

email: enquiries@openup.co.uk
world wide web: www.openup.co.uk

and

325 Chestnut Street
Philadelphia, PA 19106, USA

First published 2002

A catalogue record of this book is available from the British Library

ISBN 0 335 20851 7 (pb)   0 335 20852 5 (hb)

Library of Congress Cataloging-in-Publication Data
Edmunds, June, 1961–
    Generations, culture and society/June Edmunds and Bryan S. Turner.
      p. cm.
    Includes bibliographical references and index.
    ISBN 0-335-20852-5 – ISBN 0-335-20851-7 (pbk.)
      1. Social change.   2. Globalization – Social aspects.   3. Communication – Social aspects.   4. Culture conflict.   5. Life change events.   6. Generations.
    I. Turner, Bryan S.   II. Title.

    HM836.E368 2002
    303.4–dc21   2001058795

Typeset by Type Study, Scarborough
Printed in Great Britain by Biddles Limited, Guildford and Kings Lynn

Contents

Preface

On 11 September 2001 terrorists hijacked several American passenger aircraft and crashed two of them through the World Trade Center in Manhattan, killing thousands of civilians. The graphic images that filled the TV screens of the world were a terrible testimony to the globalization of the modern world. This date marks the creation of a new global generation, one that was shaped by the collapse of the towers in New York. Regardless of the very different interpretations and political sympathies of the people across the world who witnessed these events, their horrendous effects began to shape the consciousness of a new global generation. We might, for the sake of argument, call the generation that has been produced by these events the September generation.

An important part of our argument is that in the past traumatic events have produced distinct generations. Generations and their role in social change are best conceptualized retrospectively. It is easier to unravel the formation and impact of a past generation than to point to one in its formation. It is with hindsight that historians or sociologists can see the full force of a generation such as the 1960s generation. However, if we accept the premise that traumatic events such as warfare have been fundamentally important to the creation of generations in the past, it seems plausible to suggest that the events of 11 September will sow the seeds of a new generation created through trauma. In America, for example, the Vietnam war created a strategic generation. The terrorist attack on the World Trade Center is the most traumatic thing to have happened to America in its history. Pearl Harbor was an external threat from a known enemy. Perhaps the Civil War is on the same scale of significance. Moreover, in this particular case, people seem to be already seeing themselves as having witnessed an historic event that will remain with them forever. There is, in this respect, a sense in which history has already been chronicled. Although the ramifications of this attack are multiple, at least one of them will be the creation of a particular generation for which American isolationism will no longer be viable. Moreover, it is possible that generational trauma and cultural events have been brought together in this case. An attack on America appears to be an attack on global culture because American culture has become international.

This catastrophe therefore demonstrates an important social development, namely the rise of global generations. In historical terms, past generations were typically local and specific, but global communication makes possible the rise of a new cultural phenomenon, global generational consciousness. The development of a September generation has a number of dimensions. First, the people who fell victim to the collapsing towers were a cosmopolitan group – it included people of all age groups but who formed a particular generation because they represented a generation formed through electronic communications. Second, the nature of the work that they were doing was post-industrial, an effect of the globalization of deregulated financial services that started in the late 1970s. They were involved in managing the world economy through international banking, finance and insurance. The transactions that they made affected a wealth of nations. Third, the terrorists themselves also represented a new global generation because they emerged from a vast network whose existence and resources depended again on global forms of communication. Ironically, it was globalization itself that brought into existence an Islamic diaspora and created an anti-globalization generation. Their use of airliners, the very symbols of international travel, as weapons had great symbolic significance.

This unique tragedy can however be compared with other landslide events that entered a global consciousness. The obvious comparisons include the Vietnam war, the Kennedy assassination and the death of Diana, Princess of Wales. These events were in one sense local but through the expansion of the media they got worldwide coverage. People who lived through them continue to define their time by them, remembering exactly where they were when, for example, Kennedy was killed. So the World Trade Center has echoes of Vietnam, but it is also different. It will become the symbolic centrepiece of ongoing protest against globalization by groups who employ the technology of a global economy to undermine globalization. Because the attack has been presented as a clash between two global cultures (Islamic and western, Jihad versus McWorld), it has set in motion a new racial debate. There has been a rise in local attacks against Muslim communities in a number of countries including Britain, where mosques have become the targets for anti-religious fervour. This means that anti-globalization, whose existence was made possible by globaliz- ation, could start to destroy the possibilities for a more tolerant and benign cosmopolitanism that was brought to life initially through the growth in communications across national borders. A global 'clash of cultures' would bring to a tragic conclusion both the consumer world that has been the product of economic liberalism and the democratic cultures that were a product of the world of the baby boomers.

Our argument in this study is that generations are a critical component of social and cultural change, but their importance has been neglected in both the social sciences and humanities. We define a 'cohort' as a collec- tion of people who are born at the same time and thus share the same opportunities that are available at a given point in history. These oppor- tunities are called life chances by sociologists. A 'generation' can be defined as a cohort that for some special reason such as a major event (war, pestilence, civil conflict or natural catastrophe such as an earthquake) develops a collective consciousness that permits that generation to inter- vene significantly in social change. The post-war generation was shaped by a great variety of events – the Cold War, Vietnam, the Cuban Missile Crisis, and the rise and fall of Communism. It was also shaped by the rise of consumerism and the sexual revolution. The post-war generation was an active generation because its life chances gave it strategic advantages with respect to the economic world that opened before them. Our con- tention is that the cultural history of the western world in the second half of the twentieth century is the legacy of this large, active and problematic generation. The scale of this cultural legacy excluded the competitive emergence of later generations that have been defined by their absence – generation X or the missing generation. This hegemonic cultural leader- ship has been brought into question by the day that changed the world, because it changed the social and cultural conditions that had produced the world of the sixties generation. Traumatic historical events – the declaration of war against Hitler's Germany, the withdrawal of the

Russian army from Afghanistan, the fall of the Berlin Wall, or the New York terrorist attacks – create new forms of consciousness that transcend the divisions of class and gender to produce radical generational movements and cultures. History is the history of the consciousness of strategic, active generations.

Acknowledgements

A number of people have been instrumental in the development of the ideas that have produced this study. Mike Featherstone, Mike Hepworth and Ron Eyerman have been particularly influential through their research on consumer culture, ageing, generations, music and social movements. We should also like to thank the participants in the Cambridge conference on generational consciousness – Peter Laslett, Jackie Scott, Angela Lopez, Susan McDaniel, Peggy Watson, Molly Andrews, Johanna Esseveld, J. P. Roos, Tommi Hoikkala and Christine Minas – for their support. Finally, June would like to thank Alan Shipman for invaluable practical and intellectual support during the final stages of this project.

CHAPTER 1

Introduction: generations, war and intellectuals – towards a sociology of generations

Introduction

The importance of generations has been widely recognized in literary studies, especially in the historical understanding of the development of American literature. F. Scott Fitzgerald acknowledged the peculiar circumstances that shaped the literary imagination of the 'lost generation' of the 1920s (Berg 1981). The concept of the beat generation also recognized the specific contributions made by the circumstances of the post-war period to American literature (Charters 1992). More recently, Pierre Bourdieu (1984) has suggested that generations are causally related to changes in intellectual fashions and literary taste.

In contrast, the study of generations has not played a large part in the development of sociological theory, despite the importance of the notion of generations in common-sense or lay understanding of cultural change. Although concepts such as the 'baby boomers', the 'sixties generation', the 'generation gap' and 'generational conflict' are fundamental to popular thinking, sociology has largely neglected generation as an analytical principle. In conventional social scientific approaches, generations were either regarded as an aspect of social stratification, as a component of any general account of the ageing of populations, or as a feature of theories of social change. For example, the sociological study of social stratification was largely dominated by attempts to establish the relationships between social class, status systems, gender and ethnicity. By comparison with social class, generational inequalities and differences were regarded as relatively unimportant; though recently some authors have been trying to create a sociology of age that seeks to integrate traditional sociological variables in a seamless way with age (Ginn and Arber 1995).

In the sociology of ageing, generations were interpreted as horizontal slices within the ageing structure. The ageing of society was essentially seen to have two dimensions, namely the ageing of individuals in successive cohorts and the changing age structure of society. The sociology of ageing studied the interaction between these two processes, that is individual biography and the demographic history of society (Riley *et al.* 1988). In these studies, the analysis of generations became the study of 'cohort flows', where a 'cohort' was simply defined as the cohort of people, born in the same time period, who are ageing (Ryder 1964, 1965).

More recently, there have been debates about the impact of demographic changes that have created a large ageing population in the developed world. More specifically, these have centred around the idea of an intergenerational contract, which is based on an idea of reciprocity. That is, it is based on the notion that the contribution of the young and middle aged to supporting the elderly would be repaid when they themselves got older. In recent years, there have been arguments, coming mainly from the US, that this contract is no longer based on reciprocity. Rather, it is based on a conflict model (workers versus pensioners) where the younger generation is thought to be carrying an excessive burden to meet the resource needs of the elderly population. However, others have suggested that these ideas have been overstated and could, ultimately, be damaging to the aged (see Walker 1996; Phillipson 1998).

Alternatively, generations appeared as a specific feature of social histories or accounts of social change. Within this category, there were a number of brilliant studies on the impact of specific generations on social change such as Theweleit's (1987) analysis of the generational effects of the First World War on the subsequent rise of fascism and Mayer's (1988) exploration of the impact of the Second World War on the life chances of German survivors born between 1900 and 1930. Then there have been other various historical studies of specific generations such as the generation of 1929 (Schelsky 1963) or the 1960s generation in Germany (Bude 1995) which have ably illustrated the value of the concept.

Despite the high quality of these contributions, the concept of generation has not been developed as a powerful tool of sociological analysis. One exception was, possibly, the classic study by S. N. Eisenstadt (1956) who, in *From Generation to Generation*, applied a functionalist perspective to study how culture is transmitted through age groups. Another exception, and one of the best illustrations of intellectual change from the point of view of generations is Randall Collins's (1998) historical and comparative analysis of major intellectual figures from China, India, Japan, Greece, Islam, medieval Christendom and modern Europe. Collins shows that intellectual generations tend to have a tightly bounded lifespan, lasting, on average, thirty-three years. After this, a new adult generation replaces the previous cohort. We are applying a similar paradigm here but from a perspective rooted in Bourdieu's (1988, 1993a) thinking. Moreover, we focus particularly on the role of trauma (such as warfare, occupation or migration) in creating intellectual generations whose work stems somehow from their experience of rootlessness.

However, since the 1980s the traditional emphases of sociology have shifted, giving rise to interest in a whole range of 'post-materialist' issues. This trend has led some sociologists to suggest that class is no longer a useful analytical category (see Lee 1996: 245). The erosion of a strong class theory has, consequently, provided an opportunity to reconsider generations, especially in relation to politics and cultural change. It is against this background that a new focus on generation seems particularly pertinent. The latest concerns of sociology have provided greater opportunities for exploring generation as a further collective identity deserving of attention as a way of understanding contemporary society (Corsten 1999: 249–50). Moreover, there has been a range of external developments that are compelling sociology to address more directly the role of generations in social change.

First, the size and strategic location of the post-war generation has proved to be an important and highly visible aspect of social change in the twentieth century. In cultural and political terms, the social consequences of the baby boomers or sixties generation could not be ignored. There is general agreement that this generation has played an especially important part in transforming the social, cultural and political climate of the contemporary world. Wattenberg (1986) has shown that the American baby boomer generation was important in transforming a range of social norms, including family composition and living arrangements. Gibson (1993) has suggested that the baby boomers' adulthood has, uniquely,

4 GENERATIONS, CULTURE AND SOCIETY

been characterized by dramatic social changes including enhanced contraceptive choices, secularization, the women's movement, an increasingly technological- and service-orientated workforce and the shift toward a global economy, and that previous generations have not been subjected to such entrenched transformations. Turner (1991) has shown how attitudes towards divorce, work and family have been affected by changes in religious attitudes. Survey data suggest that the moral influence of religion is diminishing in this post-war generation (Mol 1985: 143). The retrospective debate about the 1960s, particularly by critics of the alleged excesses of popular culture, is in fact an attempt to evaluate the cultural and social impact of the post-war generation who came to maturity in the 1970s (Bloom 1987).

Second, the post-war generation was constitutive of the rise of modern consumerism, where generational audiences appear to be as important as social class or ethnic divisions or even more so. With the collapse of mass society as a consumer category, marketing and advertising are specifically structured around niche markets, of which generation is the most significant. Trends in fashion are heavily influenced by generational lifestyle. These changes in consumption are associated, in some sociological arguments, with the decline of social class as a marker of social location. The youth movement has been an important cause of such cultural changes. The speed of change in the market of youth fashion is driven by generational turnover rather than class membership (Bourdieu 1993a: 94–102). In the light of social and political changes in the market place, the sociology of youth that was established in the post-war period is starting to be reconceptualized as the sociology of generations (Lagree 1992).

Third, the demographic changes associated with the growth of an ageing population have precipitated debates about economic growth and political change. Governments have been forced to examine various welfare policies for populations that are now living much longer than previously and the question of social responsibility for these groups. The global implications of ageing are central to strategic thinking about economic growth and military power and these changes are themselves connected with the consequences of the reproductive pattern of the post-war generation (Peterson 1999). There have been growing concerns about intergenerational conflict resulting from the possibility that the current generation of older people has available to it more public resources than later generations (Vincent 1999: 103). This issue is widespread in the western world, where studies seem to be consistently showing that conflicts between the post-war generation and the younger generations are being exacerbated (Baudelot and Establet 1998; Chauvel 1998).

The notion of a 'we generation' is a consequence of these political problems that are concerned with the future funding of the welfare state. The popular notion that the post-war generation was 'selfish' raises more general questions about fairness and transfers of wealth between generations. As a consequence, generations are a necessary feature of any discussion of justice and responsibility, and have been enshrined in the Rawlsian concept of fairness (Rawls 1971: 107). A responsible generation is one that husbands its resources such that the chances of subsequent generations are not significantly diminished by the selfish actions of contemporaries. Intergenerational exchanges of income and culture create tensions within the family between conflicting loyalties over different cohorts of children (Coleman 1990).

However, one of the most important reasons for focusing on generations is rooted in the rise of globalization. When Mannheim wrote his essay (1997a) the possibilities for communication between generations across nations was very limited. This is why his focus was largely on national generations. However, because of globalization generations today cut across national boundaries in a way Mannheim could not have envisaged. It may well be that the 1960s generation was the first truly global generation in the sense that it had a common experience of global consumerism, global music and communication systems. The influence of this generation was particularly significant because it had the opportunity to transmit its message globally. This was the period when rock and roll music, which had started to take a hold in the US, was taken to Europe largely through television and, later, the trend was reversed with British groups (such as the Beatles and the Rolling Stones) exploiting American traditions but influencing audiences over there (Watts 1975: 123–39). The idea of global interdependence seems to have stemmed from this decade. Writing in the 1960s Marshall McLuhan introduced this concept and in *Understanding Media* (1964) he argued that there had been a dramatic shift from the mechanical forms of communication to electronic forms, which meant that, in an unprecedented way, culture and knowledge could be transmitted across the globe. As a way of describing this new cultural phenomenon McLuhan invented the idea of the 'global village'.

The concept of generation

There is widespread confusion surrounding the concept of generation in the sociological literature, with sociologists using it in a number of different ways. Generation has been used to represent a position within a continuum of kinship descent; as a synonym for a birth cohort such as the baby boomers; as a synonym for life stage such as 'the student generation' or to mark a historical period, that is, a cultural generation (Elder and Pellerin 1998: 264–94). Moreover, there has been a tendency to conflate four analytically distinct types of phenomena: age and life course effects; cohort or generational effects; historical trend; and period effects. The kinship concept turns on the idea that generations occur within the familial setting whereby one generation consists of a person and their siblings and the next generation is made up of that person's children and their siblings. This conception of generation is typically used to explore socialization and the diffusion of values inside the family (Miller 2000: 25–9). It has also been particularly influential in the study of political attitudes (see Braungart and Braungart 1986: 213).

In epistemological terms, there are two broad approaches to the definition of 'generation'. The first defines 'generation' as a cohort of individuals who are born at a given time. This type of definition concentrates on the specific chronological location of a generation. Generation in the sense of cohort goes beyond the familial setting. It refers to groups of people born during a specific period and who are distinct from other groups of people born in a different period, encapsulated in the contrast between a 'before time period' and an 'after time period'. According to this understanding, cohorts may be established in two ways: first demographically and/or second by historical experiences that affect a group of people born at a particular time more directly than others (Miller 2000: 30–1). We refer to this form of generational stratification as a 'cohort', namely an age group as defined by a specific point in time. Cohort analysis is thus a familiar methodological strategy in demography or the sociology of education, where statistical measures are developed for the development of social policy with respect to differences between cohorts.

However, this approach does not fully capture the forms of questions that excite sociologists. There are two particularly interesting issues. First, the social formation of distinct generations in terms of the emergence of generational cultures and politics. And second, the study of the transmission of such cultures and consciousness. A sociology of generations involves the study of generational cultures and consciousness where the specific date of a cohort may be less important than the general historical setting of generations. For example, children born in the 1980s may have a strong cultural attachment to the protest cultures of the 1960s and identify with the postwar culture of the sixties generation. There is then a further analogy between the phenomenon of class and that of generation. Just as a class ideology may, in epochs favourable to it, exercise an appeal beyond the 'location' which is proper to its habitat, certain impulses particular to a generation may, if the trend of the times is favourable to them, also attract individual members of earlier or later age groups (Mannheim 1997a: 308). Thus, the ideals and attitudes, while formulated within a particular generational cohort, can often gain acceptance over a broad social spectrum of that society and this can occur in earlier or later age groups if the ideas and trends are deemed attractive to them. Depending on the salience of events occurring around them, however, the older generation may become increasingly influenced by the social events and processes of the current dynamic generational cohort (Riggs and Turner 2000: 74–5).

There is then a need to integrate cohort and generational analysis in order to understand the importance of social resources and the strategic importance of historical circumstance. The historical impact of different generations on society is in part a consequence of their specificity, that is their particular location in the development of a society or culture. The temporal location of a cohort is important in terms of the opportunities, chances and resources that happen to be available to them. People born in Britain in 1890, 1920 and 1945 were confronted in their youth with radically different issues and life chances simply by virtue of their date of birth. But the social processes that shaped the generation of the trenches, the depression and the post-war boom are not simply determined factually by a specific time. In a general sense, we may define a generation as an age cohort that comes to have social significance by virtue of constituting itself as cultural identity. It is the interaction between historical resources, contingent circumstances and social formation that makes 'generation' an interesting sociological category. A political generation, moreover, is distinctive in its rejection of the status quo and its attempts to overturn current political values usually in response to historical circumstances (Braungart and Braungart 1986: 217–18).

The classical tradition

Classical sociology did in fact consider the relationship between age and social structures. For example Auguste Comte looked at the relationship between generational progression and progress. Karl Marx and Friedrich Engels explored the potential impact of industrialization on the significance of age and Emile Durkheim reflected on connections between age and social integration (Hagestad 1999: 514). Although these classical theorists all reflected on the social implications of age, any account of the sociology of generations characteristically starts with Karl Mannheim's pathbreaking essay on generations. 'The problem of generations' (1997a) created a promising basis for a sociology of generations and has been extensively analysed (Kertzer 1983; Longhurst 1989; Pilcher 1994; Corsten 1999). Essentially, Mannheim's discussion of generation sprang from his more general criticism of the Marxist tradition of class analysis and what he saw as its deterministic approach to consciousness or knowledge. Rejecting a monocausal account of historical change, Mannheim focused on the way age groups could act as agents of social change and become 'the carriers of intellectual and organizational alternatives to the status quo'. He therefore conceptualized generations as sources of opposition, challenging existing societal norms and values and bringing about social change through collective generational organization (Laufer and Bengtson 1974: 186).

Generation is therefore a specific component in Mannheim's sociology of knowledge. In his essay generational 'site' refers to the opportunities that are presented to a particular generation as a result of the constellation of factors that were present at its inception. A generation has specific life chances that derive from the peculiarity of its location in time. Mannheim emphasized the importance of historical process and consciousness in his definition of generations. The members of a generation are held together by the fact that they experience historical events from the same, or a similar, vantage point. He referred to this phenomenon of a common experience as the 'stratification of experience' [*Erlebnisschichtung*] (Mannheim 1997a: 297). He conceived of this stratification as a dynamic process in the formation of generational consciousness. As a result, the transmission of a common cultural heritage is always reflexive, interactive and precarious. The problem of cultural transmission is that the stratified experience of an older generation does not correspond to the experiences of a younger generation. The conflict between generations is, however, masked by the fact that intergenerational changes are continuous.

For Mannheim, generation is a category that has an existence over and above its members' awareness or consciousness of it. This is summarized in the notion of generational 'location'. In this sense, Mannheim compares generational location with class location in that members of a given class occupy an objective class position regardless of subjective awareness of it. Yet generational location is essentially a passive category, referring simply to exposure to the same historical or cultural circumstances by an age cohort. Involvement in a common destiny is not enough to define a generation. In contrast, for Mannheim, generation as an active category is encapsulated in his notion of generation as 'actuality'. He suggested that a generation becomes an 'actuality' only when 'a concrete bond is created between members of a generation by their being exposed to the social and intellectual symptoms of a process of dynamic de-stabilisation' (Mannheim 1997a: 303). Generations emerge as social effects of traumatic and violent social changes such as those brought about by Napoleon in France and Germany.

However, these forms of generational consciousness are not necessarily homogeneous or coherent because there can be distinctive divisions within a generation, defined as 'generation units'. According to Mannheim,

> Within any generation there can exist a number of differentiated, antagonistic generation-units. Together they constitute an 'actual' generation precisely because they are oriented toward each other, even though only in the sense of fighting one another. Those who were young about 1810 in Germany constituted one actual generation whether they adhered to the then current version of liberal or conservative ideas. But in so far as they were conservative or liberal, they belonged to different units of that actual generation.
>
> (Mannheim 1997a: 306–7)

Mannheim therefore used the term 'generation unit' as a way of dealing with the problem of subgroups and subdivisions within an age cohort. He suggested that any number of generation units might exist within a given generation. Thus,

> Youth experiencing the same concrete historical problems may be said to be part of the same actual generation; while those groups within the same actual generation which work up the material of their common experiences in different specific ways, constitute separate generation units.

These units are held together by 'an identity of responses' (Mannheim 1997a: 304–6) and a generation can be composed of a number of different and conflicting ensembles of generation units. This can be summed up in his notion of 'asynchronicity of contemporaries' which refers to the wealth of biographical contrasts, resulting from migration for example, in any given historical period (Weyman 1995).

The notion of generational unit can be useful to understanding contemporary generational movements. For example, Whalen and Flacks (1989) used the idea of intragenerational differences to explore the extent to which remaining members of the sixties generation identified with the era. Their research cast doubt on the idea of a coherent and continuing generational identity, showing instead that there were a number of distinctive groups or 'generation units' in this generation. Klatch (1999) has also used it to show that the popularly held notion of the 1960s being an era of exclusively left-wing activism is unfounded. Rather, she shows that the popular image neglects the anti-communist activities of the decade and, further, that the generational cohorts were divided by gender. This idea can also be usefully applied to youth movements elsewhere and at different times. In the post-war period in Britain working-class youth shared common experiences as a generation, but there were important divisions between 'mods' and 'rockers' who thus formed generation units and exhibited distinctive lifestyles. Their seasonal confrontations in British sea-side resorts further strengthened their sense of difference (Cohen 1972).

There are then three building blocks that provide the foundation of Mannheim's theory of generations. A 'generational location' is a cluster of opportunities or life chances that constitute the 'fate' of a generation. There emerges a 'generation as actuality' that shares a set of historical responses to its location and then within a generation there are generation units which articulate structures of knowledge or a consciousness that express their particular location. Generations that process a historical consciousness of their situation have the opportunity to exercise a decisive role in historical change. As a result, the 'collectively shared assumptions of a common life experience, and of a common time frame, turns into a social fact of itself' (Corsten 1999: 253).

What emerged from Mannheim's treatment of generations was clearly the problem of how generations acquire social solidarity as a consequence of shared experiences and the emergence of a collective world-view. This problem was parallel to the distinction between a class-in-itself and a class-for-itself, namely how classes become historical actors. Maurice Halbwachs (1992) provided one answer to the problem of collective memory. He applied the cultural sociology of Durkheim to the problem of social continuity through the notion of a collective memory. Durkheim, especially in *The Elementary Forms of the Religious Life* (1954), explained social solidarity through the study of rituals, which, by re-enacting the historical myths of the social group, brought about powerful emotions of social involvement. Halbwachs adapted this framework to explain the continuity of social groups such as generations through the institutionalization of collective memory. In the case of Christianity, the collective memory was stored in its doctrines, but doctrines require the social assistance of rituals if they are to be effective as transmitters of common culture. Ritual practice is the dynamic expression of common beliefs. In a similar fashion, generations become effective social networks when their social history becomes celebrated by vibrant rituals. For example, remembrance days and the ubiquitous poppy have become important for the commemoration of those generations that were sacrificed in world wars. Commemoration is an important feature of generation building through the celebration of common experiences (Schwartz 1982). Paul Connerton (1989) has similarly suggested that social memory depends upon the constant repetition of cultural habits and rituals that, by virtue of commemorative celebrations, create the sense of a public past (Lass 1994). Generations are therefore constructed through the institutionalization of memory through collective rituals and narratives (Eyerman and Turner 1998).

These studies turn on the question of how culture is transformed and transmitted across generations. Sociological research on generations has typically focused on the mechanisms by which culture (the collective memory) is transferred by socialization and the internalization of culture (see Eisenstadt 1956). Social breakdown occurs when culture is inadequately carried through the social structure and age groups fail to inculcate the dominant culture. In fact, the failure of cultural transmission appears as a more or less permanent feature of modern societies where there has been an explosion of technological knowledge and secular culture such that age is no longer a feature of stable relations of authority. In the context of building and maintaining institutions, unsuccessful transmission of culture would appear to be normal in an advanced society and hence the theme of the rebelliousness of new generations is a persistent aspect of social tensions (Berger and Luckmann 1966: 76).

In England, John Osborne's *Look Back in Anger* and films such as *The L-Shaped Room* were influential statements about the values and lifestyle of a post-war generation that could not accept the culture of pre-war Britain (Marwick 1998: 136). The British poet Philip Larkin, whose poetry was inspired by the conservatism of the 1950s, regarded aspects of 1960s culture as essentially subversive (see Marwick 1998: 8). In America, Jack Kerouac's *On the Road* (1958) employed the metaphor of motoring through America to explore the alienation of youth in a society where material values and consumerism were transforming the traditional culture of post-war American society. It is possible to speculate that intergenerational conflict and misunderstanding are inevitable features of a society where social change is a rapid, ineluctable and permanent feature of a technological civilization (Turner 1998).

Traumatic events: developments in life course research

Research on generations by Mannheim and Halbwachs established the basic contours of the sociology of generations in terms of the importance of shared cultures and rituals that constituted the collective memory of a generation. It is clear that this research tradition was itself heavily influenced by the historical context. For example, Mannheim was acutely aware of the problems of German youth and the political instability of values and structure in central Europe. The rise of fascism was itself partly the product of alienated youth generations after the catastrophe of the First World War. Mannheim escaped from revolutionary Hungary in 1919, then fled from Germany in 1933 to escape National Socialism and eventually settled in Britain where he became a professor at the London School of Economics. Mannheim's life illustrates the disruptions and crises of Europe in the first half of the twentieth century. These traumatic events – two world wars, the Holocaust, the Russian Revolution, the Spanish Civil War, the creation of the state of Israel, and post-war global migration – were constitutive of experiences that sharply divided societies into distinctive generations. It is hardly surprising that Mannheim was interested in 'the problem of generations'.

A generation can be defined in terms of a collective response to a traumatic event or catastrophe that unites a particular cohort of individuals into a self-conscious age stratum. The traumatic event uniquely cuts off a generation from its past and separates it from the future. The event becomes the basis of a collective ideology and a set of integrating rituals that become the conduit for the commemoration of the traumatic experience. The principal illustration is the experience of trench warfare that ushered in the age of mechanical violence and seared the consciousness of a generation (Wohl 1979). Post-colonial societies also provide good examples of cohort generations defined by watershed transformations. In such cases three generational cohorts can be distinguished: the generation that grew up in the pre-independence colonial system; the generation that took part in the struggle for independence; and the generation that was born and grew up in the post-independence era (Miller 2000: 33).

The traumatic events that shaped generations in the twentieth century were associated with war. While the First World War shaped the consciousness of men, the Second World War had equally traumatic effects for civilians, especially women. The Spanish Civil War had a profound impact on the division of generations between right and left, while the Vietnam war deeply divided America along generational lines. However, a traumatic event in shaping generational consciousness does not have to be about warfare. An important feature of the growth of generational studies has been research on the Depression. The development of generational or life course research has been significantly shaped by the research of Glen Elder in, for example, *Children of the Great Depression: Social Change in*

Life Experience (1974). Elder's research specifically focused on how people survive trauma and, while it permanently shapes their lives, how they triumph over adversity. He has conceptualized the impact of the life course in terms of four key elements: location in time and place, the mediation of social relations (or 'linked lives'), the intersection of age, period and cohort timing, and finally the development of the individual in terms of human agency. Elder's work is a clear illustration both of the improvement of research methodologies in generational research and of the growth of a body of concepts relating to generations (Giele and Elder 1998). Because Elder was primarily concerned with the triumph of individuals over the adversities of historical accident (being born in the wrong place at the wrong time), his research brings clearly into view the interaction between biography and history.

Pierre Bourdieu and generations

While Mannheim (1997a) provided the starting point for studies of generations, his thinking alone cannot illuminate how cohorts of intellectual generations emerge and the generational rivalry that acts as a catalyst for paradigm shifts. To address this concern, it would be useful to link some of Mannheim's insights with those of other theorists, in particular those of Pierre Bourdieu (1988, 1993b). The most notable interpretations of Bourdieu's thinking have generally ignored the importance of generation as an explanatory factor in Bourdieu's account of cultural change, focusing instead on the role of class (Jenkins 1992; Chaney 1996; Fowler 1997). Bourdieu's work is relevant to the study of generations and culture because, although class position appears to determine the broad parameters of taste and value within each cultural field, generational struggle seems to be especially important in major ruptures in taste and practice.

Bourdieu's discussion of generations is dispersed through his work and there is no integration of his commentary into a theory of generational change. However, his most systematic commentary on generations can be found in the essays on youth in *Sociology in Question* (Bourdieu 1993a). Like Mannheim (1997a) Bourdieu treats the problem of generation as an alternative to class in explanations of social change, especially rapid and regular change, as in art fashion. First, generational struggles are significant in relation to intellectual change and conflict between generations for ownership of cultural capital in, for example, *Homo Academicus* (Bourdieu 1988). Second, in the analysis of cultural changes in terms of artistic generations in *The Field of Cultural Production* (Bourdieu 1993b) and *The Rules of Art* (Bourdieu 1996), struggles between age cohorts seem to be vital. Third, there are similar arguments with respect to 'ancients' and 'moderns' in *In Other Words: Essays Towards Reflexive Sociology* (Bourdieu 1990b), and finally, there is the notion of generational conflict that makes a brief appearance in *Reproduction in Education, Society and Culture* (Bourdieu and Passeron 1990).

In an analysis that complements Mannheim's approach, Bourdieu starts an extended discussion of generations by asserting that they are socially, not biologically, produced. For example, 'youth and age are not self evident data, but are socially constructed, in the struggle between youth and the old' (Bourdieu 1993a: 95). In the same place, when seeking to understand the divisions between age groups, he writes that one has to 'know the specific laws of functioning of the field'. Further, the antagonisms between generations are 'clashes between systems of aspirations formed in different periods' (Bourdieu 1993a: 99). Different levels of the system of society shape these aspirations, expectations and tastes. Thus, the field of generational conflicts is shaped by educational credentials and by conflicts over different socialization practices.

Bourdieu therefore interprets the student conflicts of 1968 as clashes between different generational cohorts within higher education. These struggles of French students were about academic generations that were produced by the educational system itself within a specific historical context. Thus,

> Contrary to what was thought and written at the time of the crisis of May 1968, the conflict which divided the faculties did not oppose generations understood in the sense of age but academic generations, that is agents, who, even when they are the same age, have been produced by two different modes of academic 'generation'.
>
> (Bourdieu 1988: 147)

In other words, by academic cohorts that were 'generated' in distinct economic and social circumstances. These struggles were in fact, he argues, over the cultural scarcities that are the product of academic recruitment, advancement and promotion.

Finally, Bourdieu maintains that the rate of change in the cultural sphere is an effect of the intensity of the struggle for scarce cultural resources between generational groups. In *The Field of Cultural Production*, Bourdieu (1993b) argues that in France there has been from the 1830s onwards an endless struggle between avant-garde and bourgeois art, between left bank and right bank, between young and old, for artistic hegemony. The maintenance of a distinction between being fashionable and out of fashion requires a constant revolution in taste, cultural objects and genres. Artistic change is a function of generational conflicts over scarcity, which is in turn produced by the competitive structure of educational systems. Although this approach could be described as reductionist given its emphasis on conflict over resources, it nevertheless broadens out conflict to include generations. Bourdieu suggested that artistic change, for example, could be understood in the following way. Age cohorts of artists and intellectuals develop a generational habitus through their struggle for recognition on the cultural field, because the major weapon in this struggle is the form and content of art works; there is here an inbuilt process of innovation and change. These changes are rapid and their specific forms and contents cannot be easily predicted, or even understood sociologically.

One of the problems arising from Bourdieu's thinking on generations is the continuing tension between cohort and sociological analysis, that is between treating generations as naturally occurring phenomena (age groups) and as socially occurring phenomena (social groups) (Bourdieu 1993a: 95). This discussion of how generations shape cultural capital in different social formations shows that Bourdieu has two contradictory views of generations. His dominant view is that they are categories for structuring social relations (in this sense they are socially constructed). Thus, in his treatment of intergenerational conflicts between intellectuals in *Homo Academicus* (Bourdieu 1988), he suggests that intellectual generations are defined by educational categories and he highlights the importance of specific historical conjunctures. However, he also appears to argue that generations are real cohorts of people in the population structure passing through time. For example, in his discussion of youth in *Sociology in Question* (1993a) he treats generations as real groups of young people. While he argues that 'youth' is a social category that is an effect of struggles between the young and the old, he also is implicitly forced to recognize 'the young' and 'the old' as age groups, the struggle between which produces a recognized social category of 'youth'.

Bourdieu's sociological approach has therefore produced a set of concepts that are relevant to our study. Briefly, a generation becomes a significant social force if its members share a common habitus. The traumatic event has to be incorporated into the practices of the everyday world of a generation and thus to structure its habitus. It is possible to argue further that a powerful generational habitus becomes embodied in the social actors who are carriers of such cultures. Their dress, speech and deportment come to embody the history and experience of a particular generation, that can recognize its members through their special form of presentation of self, namely the manner in which they embody a generational code. We often attribute parenthood to people by observing the inheritance of biology across generations when we note how children resemble their parents. The solidarity of a generation can be measured by the effective transmission and maintenance of a habitus of gestures, presentations and modes of action by its members. The habitus is the collection of practices through which generational experiences are manifest.

Where a generation manages to develop a strong sense of its own culture through a shared habitus, it has a greater ability to mobilize its members around political issues or social causes. We might argue that the post-war baby boomers have retained a liberal culture and a habitus that is hostile to formal codes of behaviour. The early stages of the development of this generation were associated with radical social movements and these experiences shaped its culture. A generation that has a strong consciousness and maintains its social solidarity has the capacity to act in politics, and to meet the contingencies and exigencies of its particular historical location. The parallel with social classes is obvious in the sense that a solidaristic generation is a generation for-itself, and has the capacity to mobilize to transform societies in conformity with its own constellation of interests. In short, we can distinguish between active and passive generations.

Because we want to write in part a social history of generational cohorts, their consciousness and the social consequences of generational politics, we are sceptical of the usefulness of social constructionism as an epistemology. However, as we have indicated, individuals may frequently identify with generational cultures to which they are not chronologically connected (this is why the 1960s is such a powerful social concept). Nevertheless, the way individuals identify or not is an empirical question. We therefore suggest that this way of approaching generations (in terms of their politics/consciousness) is much more interesting than the typical location of generations in the sociology of ageing where generation is a cohort in a population structure (see Riley 1987; Pilcher 1994, 1995).

Active and passive generations

In this book we aim to connect generations with intellectual, cultural and national consciousness through a distinction between active and passive generations. This distinction touches on the etymological significance of 'generation' from 'to generate'. Active generations make a generative contribution to a social community or polity rather than passively accept a given culture. Whether or not a generation produces a new or different cultural heritage is closely connected with the strategic opportunities that are present in a specific period. The creative contribution to popular culture that was the legacy of the post-war generation was made possible by the post-war demographic explosion that produced the baby boomers, the emergence of post-war affluence, the expansion of the educational system and the presence of small but significant bits of technology – record players, the scooter and the contraceptive pill.

This conception of active and passive generations follows the approach of David Wyatt (1993) in his *Out of the Sixties*. In his discussion of how a generation is constituted Wyatt prioritizes a number of factors. First, he suggests that traumatic events such as wars play a formative part in the creation of generations because they provide an historical watershed and a shared sense of distress. Second, he stresses the importance of mentors in generational consciousness, claiming that generations tend to identify with notable mentors, that is, groups of dissenters from the dominant culture who lead the opposition to establishment, for example, the Beats or Malcolm X or Martin Luther King. Third, he maintains that demographic change is important to the formation of generations (for example, the loss of people through wars or catastrophes or through a boom in births such as the post-war baby boom). Fourth, he refers to the 'privileged interval', which refers to the way generations develop not just out of the period in which they experience decisive events but also in the previous and subsequent periods that 'bracket' them. Fifth, generations are constituted through 'sacred places', that is, particular geographical localities take on a symbolic and long-lasting place in the collective memories of a given generation such as Woodstock and Paris for the sixties generation. Finally, through the idea of the 'happy few' Wyatt suggests that generations include people who provide each other with mutual support and reinforcement and recognize each other as genuine members of a given generation (Wyatt 1993: 2–4).

Within the notion of an active generation, it is possible to specify further the development of a *strategic* generation. Rather like individuals, not all generations capitalize on the resources and opportunities that are presented to them. A strategic generation is one that, given a condition or set of objectively favourable circumstances, can create a potent generational consciousness or ideology of political change that is sufficient to bring about significant social change. The political force of a strategic generation is measured by the fact that its world-view significantly conditions the circumstances of subsequent generations. A strategic generation is generative of the conditions of thinking and action of subsequent cohorts. In Marxist terminology, it is a generation for-itself. We distinguish between passive and active generations, arguing that social change may be brought about by the contingently available strategic advantages of a generational cohort plus the consolidation of moral or hegemonic leadership. War and its social consequences have been a particularly important lever for the formation of generational consciousness and leadership. The strategic impact of a self-conscious generational cohort provides a dividing line between passive (in-itself) generations and active or strategic (for-itself) generations.

Finally, it could be sociologically interesting to reflect on historical change in terms of a rotation between passive and active generations (parallel to a Pareto-type circulation of elites). Successful strategic generations will be reluctant to surrender their historical advantages to a rising generation, thereby creating a lag in social opportunity. This model of social circulation was in fact explicit in Mannheim's (1997b) view of rising and declining social classes in his contrast between ideology and utopia. In his application of this model in his analysis of conservative thought, Mannheim attempted to show that the conservative imagination is characteristic of a social class in opposition to the modernist project of industrial capitalism, but also the thought of a social class in decline (Mannheim 1997c). Romanticism and historicism were different phases of conservative thought that in various ways rejected the social changes brought about by capitalism.

There are therefore two general processes that become theoretically salient. First, strategic generations will conservatively attempt to retain control over social and cultural resources, thereby constraining the opportunities of the next generation. Second, there is an oscillation between generations, whereby an out-group perceives an incumbent generation as necessarily conservative, precisely because an incumbent generation attempts to conserve its resources. The dynamic relationship between generations is structured by the processes of social closure that were defined in Max Weber's analysis of social stratification in terms of class, status and party. As Frank Parkin has pointed out (1979), communal status groups based on social closure are resilient social units that cut across class defined in economic terms.

Generational conflict takes place when there is an over-production of talented people with respect to a number of socially finite positions forcing them to innovate to survive in the cultural field (Mulkay and Turner 1971). According to this perspective the baby boomers, the cohort born between 1945 and 1950, are the 'lucky generation' by virtue of being the first cohort to grow up in a largely peaceful and affluent post-war society. Moreover, the fact that this cohort was demographically so large has enabled it to form a powerful culture with new lifestyles, tastes and social mores. The generation following them, however, has been disadvantaged by the comparative lack of opportunities providing scope for conflict in, for example, the labour market. It may well be that contemporary changes in the economy have heightened generational conflict. Tensions between the older and younger generation in the labour market are becoming more and more marked as the younger generation has to face growing job insecurity resulting from the increasingly flexible character of the labour market. Some studies of intergenerational relations among women in America have, for example, found that instead of relations of reciprocity forming, intergenerational rivalry has emerged as the older generation feels resentment at having put into place the very structures that are enabling younger women to enjoy the benefits of both career and family (Moreno and Murphy 1999).

Clearly, generations are not social classes because their members are recruited from different social classes. Generations are not status groups as such; but different generations have specific status characteristics. Finally, generations, like competitive status groups and classes, enter into a field of social struggle because the transmission of social resources through time is not wholly regulated by law and is necessarily character-ized by conflict. Although this comment could be regarded as the begin-ning of a more systematic theory of generations, it does clarify a central point of this study. The Mannheimian 'problem of generations' is essen-tially a problem of social scarcity in the context of the transmission and allocation of economic, social and cultural resources over time. More briefly, generation as a principle of social stratification involves the structuring of resources by social cohorts through time.

As we have already suggested, generational responses to particular trau-mas may well not be unified or homogeneous. For example, it was the question of how people could have lived through the same set of dramatic events and interpreted them in such radically different ways that moti-vated Klatch's (1999) analysis of the 'sixties generation'. Finding that the literature on the 1960s used Mannheim's ideas without considering the notion of intra-generational conflict Klatch set out to challenge the com-monly held image of the 1960s generation as unified and to explore the divisions within it. She showed that the association between this decade and left-wing politics has obscured the role of right-wing (youth) activists as well as ignoring women's experience of the decade. Not only then did Klatch explore internal generational cohorts in terms of their location on the political spectrum, she also looked at how these subgroups were divided by gender.

The neglect of intra-generational consciousness has been a typical feature of existing studies, with the literature on political generations tending to ignore gender as a variable and consequently denying that women and men may differently experience significant historical events, such as wars, that bound cohort analyses (Schneider 1988: 10). A notable exception to this trend is Scott's work on generations and gender (see Scott 2000). Other generational divisions, such as ethnicity, have also been neglected. As we have already suggested, generational responses to particular traumas may well not be unified or homogeneous. Different strata within a cohort generation may have very different collective memories. That is, variables such as gender, class or ethnicity are likely to make generational units experience the same events in different ways. For example, combat soldiers in Vietnam were predominantly working-class and disproportionately black and 'hippies' tended to come from privileged backgrounds (Braungart and Braungart 1986: 217; Miller 2000: 33–4).

This is why in this study we are also interested in exploring generational consciousness through the notion of generation units following Mannheim. This is important because of the need to rectify the imbalance discussed above. The relationships between these generational subgroups have been under-theorized. An important question is under what circumstances does generational consciousness become most salient? It has been suggested that generational identity becomes more salient in the absence of non-generational factors such as racial, class or sexual subordination (Laufer and Bengtson 1974: 188). However, it may be that the salience of categories such as class, gender, ethnicity or age can vary at different historical moments (Eyerman and Turner 1998: 99) and that generation has become more salient in the light of the historical, demographic and global changes mentioned earlier.

What is needed then is a book that introduces new ways of looking at generations theoretically and carries out this examination in relation to highly topical substantive issues that are also central to contemporary sociology. In this study, we aim to develop a programmatic theory of generations in order to make the concept more central to sociological analysis and understanding. Our strategy is to use a historical/comparative approach with trauma as the main constitutive factor – and this is how it differs from traditional generational approaches. The key theme is the transformative experience of war and uprooting. The Second World War led to more dislocation; these events divided off generations in a way that transcended class. The historical studies of the impact of the traumatic experiences on life course have made an important contribution to historical understanding and the growing literature on political generations has provided an interesting insight into the way political ideologies are created. We are interested also in the question of generational consciousness as a strategy for bringing about change.

This book offers a theoretically innovative way of examining generational consciousness through a reinterpretation of Mannheim's (1997a) thinking on intellectual generations and a critical examination of Bourdieu's (1988, 1993a) understanding of generational cohorts. A conceptual distinction between active and passive generations will be introduced as a way of exploring social and cultural change. Because generation is as significant as social class our discussion of it here necessarily has to be limited to specific issues. We are therefore concentrating on the relationship between generations, intellectuals, culture and nationalism. Moreover, because we agree with the idea that generation is typically formed by traumatic events, we are concentrating on the impact of warfare in particular on intellectual generations and national consciousness. In the twentieth century, the Second World War and the Vietnam war have been especially significant; we are therefore looking at the question through generational 'slices'. For example, in relation to America the key is the creation of the 1960s generation and the Bloom reaction (namely, a far-ranging critique of the consequences of the 1960s politics and culture) is all part of the national crisis in America (Vietnam was the first problem faced), whereas for western Europe the Second World War has been decisive. Finally, because the peculiar impact of 1960s social movements is widely acknowledged, we pay a lot of attention to this particular generation.

Our principal goal is to demonstrate the value of generations over class in understanding cultural, intellectual and national change in the twentieth century. Thus in Chapter 2 we focus on the role of generations in cultural change through a discussion of youth culture in America, Australia and Britain. We suggest that the 1960s generation, as the first international generation, has played a particularly important role in shaping contemporary culture. Through an assessment of retrospective analyses of this period and critics such as Bloom (1987) we suggest that far from being the 'we' generation attributed by critics of the era, this generation has introduced a valuable dimension to culture, especially in areas such as multiculturalism and women's rights.

In Chapter 3 we discuss the role of generations in the intellectual field by exploring various key intellectuals from a range of backgrounds. This chapter departs from traditional conceptions of intellectuals as an expression of class structure (Antonio Gramsci and Bourdieu) and instead follows Mannheim who saw intellectuals as 'free floating'. Our argument here is that intellectuals are shaped not so much by class as by generational location. While Collins's (1998) model of generations and intellectual change looks at a much earlier period, his argument is relevant to our findings because it ends in the middle of the nineteenth century whereas we concentrate on more contemporary intellectual trends. This might be significant because it is possible to speculate that more recent generations have a shorter lifespan because of the new ways in which ideas can be transmitted. Novel ideas spread more quickly than in the past, leading to a situation where there is more overlap between generations.

We illustrate our perspective on the relationship between generation and intellectual development by considering in some detail a variety of intellectual generations from America and France. Through a discussion of developments in American intellectual thought through the Frankfurt School, the New York Intellectuals (Daniel Bell is a classic Americanized Jewish generational cohort), intellectual generations in France emerging in response to French occupation and Edward Said (who is articulating a Palestinian consciousness), we highlight the importance of the experience of war, occupation and migration on the production of intellectual generations. In this chapter we also introduce a distinction between nostalgic and utopian intellectual generations, suggesting that experience of rootlessness and disruption creates nostalgic generations, but ultimately paves the way for cosmopolitanism.

In Chapters 4 and 5 we argue that, while there is a wealth of important and insightful literature on nationalism, there has been a significant tendency to neglect the role of generations in creating and recreating national consciousness. We suggest that founding fathers, itself a generational concept, play a critical role in constructing a generational consciousness that seeks to impose cultural unity on disparate groups and constructs a national consciousness that tends to be exclusionary towards latecomers or migrants and women. However, the aim is ultimately to show that later generations of migrants and women play an important part in challenging and overturning dominant and traditional conceptions of national consciousness, paving the way for a more tolerant, open and cosmopolitan national identity. In Chapter 4 we illustrate this through a discussion of shifts in national consciousness in America and Britain and a consideration of the role of minorities in challenging primordial understandings of national identity.

In Chapter 5, we develop this theme further through an account of women's role in nationalist movements and a case study of elite British women's views on Britishness/Englishness in the context of devolution, European integration and globalization. Both chapters differ from the previous ones in that they draw on contemporary interviews with members of the 1960s generation. The aim is to show how groups from the margins, through generational change, come to play a central part in redefining national identity. In Chapter 6, the conclusion, we set out again the theoretical conclusions of our thinking on generations and outline the reasons why sociology should give generations a more central place in its field.

CHAPTER 2

Generations and culture

It is widely held that the post-war generation has had a uniquely dramatic effect on contemporary culture, especially in popular literature, and that the sixties generation in particular has had a formative impact on later practices and beliefs. The significance of this generation is indicated by the way that it continues to spark political debate and media coverage, with some deploring the consequences of this decade and others celebrating them. While the 1950s and the 1970s attract minimal attention, the 1960s 'stay hot' (Farber 1994: 1). The baby boomers (or sixties generation) are a generational cohort that has generally experienced longevity, relative peace and a large degree of economic prosperity. It was in a sense the first mass consumer generation, which created lifestyles that continue to have some nostalgic credibility. This generation was unique because it grew up in a period of particular historical significance in that the social and political upheavals characteristic of the era were unparalleled and, moreover, perceived as such by those who experienced them. As we start the new millennium, there is a widespread sense of the importance of an evaluation of the *fin de siècle* culture of late modernity, and in particular a need to assess the role and importance of various post-war generations.

Describing the sixties as a 'cultural revolution', Marwick (1998) has identified a range of key characteristics of this era. At the cultural and economic level, the sixties marked an upsurge of entrepreneurialism and individualism; it was a period of massive technological advance, manifest in the production of consumer goods such as television and records. There was a high degree of social mobility that meant that the new consumer society was open to large sections of the population. Youth became particularly important in shaping fashion, music and popular culture generally and it was a time when, through the idea of 'spectacle', new oppositional behaviours became popularly visible; there was also an important surge in international cultural exchange and a popular culture that stressed beauty, made rock music into a 'universal language' and celebrated conceptual art. At the intellectual level, the sixties facilitated new ways of thinking rooted mainly in the opposition between structuralism and post-structuralism and associated with intellectuals such as Althusser and Foucault (Marwick 1998: 17–20).

Politically the baby boomers came of age in a period of international turmoil, decolonization and, most critically, the Vietnam war. The era was distinctive in that it saw the formation of movements that tended to be anti-establishment, such as the New Left, the civil rights movement, the anti-war campaign, feminism, the nuclear disarmament peace movement and anti-colonialism. It involved shifting patterns of class, racial and familial relations as well as a new permissiveness in sexual and personal relations, and the new climate was defined in opposition to the sexual repression of the 1950s. Finally, it was the period when 'race' began to be increasingly addressed. In America, the debates turned on integration whereas in countries such as France and Britain the issue was more about the establishment of new minority communities (Marwick 1998: 17–20).

In the United States in the mid-1950s a general societal focus on 'youth' intensified through the commercial mass media, and helped coalesce a generational awareness and produce conflict around a refusal to assume the positions that society offered. Figures such as James Dean were critical to this. Dean represented the invention of the teenager, rebelling against parental authority. His persona, being both masculine and feminine at the same time, challenged conventional ideas about sexuality (Alexander 1995). This new focus on youth grew rapidly throughout the next decade. The Berkeley Free Speech Movement (FSM) of 1963 organized college youth around the issue of refusing to be moulded to fit the needs of the corporate world for which the higher education in the 'multiversities' was preparing them. This youth movement involved race, class, and gender, as well as this generational aspect. Most of those engaged in the movement, at least in its earlier stages, were middle-class and white. This rather privileged refusal, however, served as a catalyst for the much more broadly based youth movements that followed.

What characterizes the youth movements of the 1960s was the role of popular culture in their constitution. Writing about the US, Todd Gitlin (1987) focuses on rock music as a key element that solidified youth of divergent class and racial, gender and regions into a generation-in-revolt. It was especially through music and other forms of popular culture such as film – the very elements of 'mass culture' that traditional intellectuals castigated for inducing false consciousness – that a generational consciousness was solidified around the idea of an 'alternative culture'. The culture industry had helped produce its opposite. While European student movements may have been more focused around ideology, and anti-American in their outlook, they also took American popular culture as their own, from folk music to rock and roll and Hollywood films. Opposition to American imperialism and capitalism was, throughout the twentieth century, combined with mass adoption of American popular culture (Bigsby 1975).

In the 1950s, American-based jazz helped to construct a 'bohemian' alternative to the dominant culture; in the 1960s it was rock and roll, also a derivative of African American music that played the same role. In a recent history of the politics of American popular music, Brian Ward (1998) has suggested that the emergence of a market for an interracial popular music in the mid-1950s contributed to the development of the civil rights movement. The social barriers that separated blacks and whites into segregated communities were first transcended by radio and by musical tastes. Ward suggests that this new taste in music, which expressed itself first through listening and then through record purchases, forced a music industry encased in a racially divided view of its market into recording and promoting a new integrated popular music, of which rock and roll was one outcome. The reception of this music by white and black teenagers, first in segregated and then integrated audiences, predisposed at least some 'youths' to support or sympathize with the civil rights movement as it emerged. The sense of a new generation, one differently moulded from that of their elders regarding race relations, has perhaps been one of the longest lasting legacies of the 1960s in the United States.

The uniqueness of the sixties events rests also with their international character: taking in North America, Australia and much of western Europe. There was a domino effect whereby developments in America started to take a hold in countries across other parts of the world. The Vietnam war, while sparking off protest movements in America, also mobilized the student generation across western Europe, including Britain and France. And Sweden was host to the largest peace movement outside the US. By the late 1960s European intellectuals and students were on side with the American New Left (Caute 1988: 11). Other developments in America crossed the Atlantic, such as those linked with the New Left, civil rights and feminism. These trends in the United States were important to the development of feminism and a culture of sexual freedom in Britain (Lovenduski and Randall 1993: 61–2). The youth cultures that had developed in America also crossed the Atlantic, though resurfacing with peculiarly British features. By the end of the 1960s youth movements started to flourish in Britain with distinctively British class-related aspects: the Mods expressed working-class youth culture and the Rockers and hippies were an expression of middle-class youth culture (Barker 1995: 16–17).

Comparable developments took place in Australia, again with specific features that were unique to the context. Anne Coombs (1996) has provided an analysis of the 'Sydney Push', an earlier generation of intellectuals associated with the philosopher John Anderson in Sydney in the years immediately after the Second World War. Here the atmosphere of peacetime liberation produced a generation of free spirits that included, among others, Germaine Greer. Although this movement predated the 1960s, it reached its peak at this time and its intellectuals were typically anti-authority, challenging various forms of authority and establishment values generally. Coombs (1996) described the Sydney Push as a 'generation in search of freedom' (1949–57). Recruited from the post-war bohemian, university and fringe cultures of central Sydney, the Push expressed oppositional values and its membership included people such as Roelof Smilde and Darcy Waters as well as Greer. The Push produced a series of films, plays and novels that challenged the conservatism of white post-war Australian prosperity. This fact makes it all the more interesting that Greer is now herself under attack for being out of touch with the interests of younger feminists (Wallace 1997). There is as a result some degree of hostility between the 'lucky generation' and generation X. In *Gangland*, Mark Davis (1997) explores the dominance of this generation in Australia in terms of popular music, feminist politics, the media establishment and the culture industry. He concludes, 'Both the cultural and political elites have constructed a two-tier culture where younger people are on the outer, denied full participation, consistently set up as ciphers for "what is wrong" and represented as an alien race' (Davis 1997: 253).

Turning our attention to Europe, 1960s France was characterized by political unrest, with the student riots and protests against the Vietnam war as well as more directly related conflicts such as Algeria. Much of the protests turned on the question of France's colonial ties and, in particular, the Algerian question with protesters supporting independence for Algeria and later protesting against the treatment of Algerian immigrants (Marwick 1998: 534–5). The students forged an alliance with the workers against various forces of authority and a younger generation of university teachers sided with the students. Although the events were largely political, there are some suggestions that the students were not just interested in dissident political ideas but also lifestyle changes. Nevertheless, unlike in Britain, there was no home-grown pop culture. Rather the French imported people such as Joan Baez.

Similar events took place in other advanced industrial societies, contributing not only to an awareness of generational differences among contemporaries, but also to the attempts by later generations to understand their own identity. In Germany, Heinz Bude (1995) has argued that there is a strong sense of generational identity and division as constituted by attitudes, for example, towards the student movements of 1968 and the political activities surrounding student leaders such as Rudi Dutschke. In Sweden an historical re-evaluation of the largely student-based anti-Vietnam war movement has aroused considerable public interest. In England, there is currently much cultural re-evaluation in connection with such figures as Mick Jagger (Anderson 1993). The recent death of William Burroughs (Miles 1992) has encouraged a retrospective analysis of the beat generation, where even oppositional figures, like Lawrence Ferlinghetti, have become part of the post-war establishment (Silesky 1990).

In the Netherlands, current debates turn on the question of the relative success of the values of this decade. In *Building New Babylon: the Netherlands in the sixties* (1995) and *New Babylon and the Politics of Modernity* (1997) James Kennedy suggests that the social and cultural transformations that took place in the 1960s were facilitated by the elite (social, political, cultural and religious), which was particularly tolerant of the younger generation's ideas. It is argued that this is why there was little overt generational conflict in the Netherlands whereas in America, where the individualistic tradition of elites was more entrenched, there emerged a more obvious generation gap and defence of traditional values. Others have suggested that the success of the Netherlands case cannot be understood through internal politics and culture. Thus Righart (1995) has claimed that the shifts in the Netherlands were more moderate because they focused on culture rather than politics whereas in Great Britain there was a lower level of generational conflict because the country was governed by a socially progressive Labour government and a comparatively modest baby boom.

Comparative analyses of generational cultures consistently bring up accounts of generational competition, especially over cultural capital and political influence. In global terms, the American 1960s generation was crucial in establishing the contemporary framework within which generational politics and culture has to be understood. The sixties generation was produced by opposition to the Vietnam war and expressed disillusion with the previous generation's Cold War politics; it was not in tune with the political mood that produced McCarthyism. That the new generation blamed their parents for war in all its forms was encapsulated in the slogan 'Make Love not War' (Anderson 1995: 247). The broader social causes of protest were associated with the rapid increase in the numbers of students entering the public universities, the growing size of universities and the proliferation of critical social science programmes in the faculties. The spread of a critical and rebellious youth culture through the activism of university students created an enhanced awareness of the presence and importance of a 'generation gap' (Lipsitz 1994).

The historical difference between Britain and America is crucial for understanding generational differences. Whereas young Americans and Australians were brutalized by involvement in Vietnam, post-war British generations grew up in a period of affluence and relative peace. Their encounter with the Cold War was largely a passive spectator experience, and they did not live through the social divisions that followed from the Algerian Revolution, the wars in Mozambique, Vietnam or later in Afghanistan. The Malaysian emergency and the Suez crisis were local and short-term disruptions to the post-war peace. Although the Campaign for Nuclear Disarmament (CND) was an important social movement that shaped the consciousness of a generation, it did not necessarily divide the nation into hostile camps. Living in Britain in the post-war period involved watching the British state manage global decline and containment in economic, military and social terms. In this respect, the baby boomers were a passive rather than strategic generation.

A common theme in these examples is the notion that social closure operates to limit access to influential positions in a society. In order to climb up the social ladder where desirable positions in the system are limited, younger generations must compete with the establishment and they do this by innovation. Generational identities and cultures are thus produced in competitive social fields. One grounding for the historical emergence of generational conflict is the circumstance of the overproduction of talented individuals with respect to a number of socially finite positions. When this is perceived to be age-related, it can produce generational conflict because individuals entering the field will be forced to innovate in order to survive (Mulkay and Turner 1971). Where influential social positions are scarce, new generations must either vacate the field (and establish a new game) or innovate (and thereby create a new product). With the transition of the economy from Fordism to post-Fordism, there has been a profound restructuring of the occupational system with a growth in the service sector, a decline in industrial manufacturing and an increase in the number of jobs relating to communication and the leisure industries (Reich 1991). Long-term difficulties associated with structural unemployment and underemployment mean that it is difficult to see how young workers in the twenty-first century will find sufficient employment to provide them with entitlements within the welfare states. The indications are that work will become increasingly scarce, typically short-term and casual and normally unpredictable. Increased life expectancy has now been identified as a major cause of the current economic slowdown both in Japan and the west. This economic scenario is a recipe for significant industrial and social unrest in which struggles will be frequently based on generational rather than class conflicts (Turner 2000b).

Post-war generations in the UK: from violence to consumption

The experience of wars has been critical to the formation of previous generations in the UK and, more specifically, the differences between those who took part in the First World War and those who did not. In the cultural realm this division can be marked by the contrast between literary figures such as Robert Graves, Edmund Blunden and Siegfried Sassoon on the one hand and W. H. Auden, Christopher Isherwood, Stephen Spender, C. Day Lewis and Louis MacNeice on the other. Skelton (1964: 15) has pointed out that the men of the 1904–16 generation were not only deprived of the easy Georgian days, but also forced into a period of intense social tension in which to do their growing up. The older thirties men struggled through their adolescence during the last days of a war and the early confusions of an embittered peace, while the younger ones were adolescents at the time of the General Strike and the Depression. It was not possible to avoid being affected by these matters, however secure one's personal life might have been. Chartism and the Crimean War left many members of the community completely untouched, but the Great War and the Depression left their mark on every inch of the country.

Despite these differences, social theory and the literary imagination were dominated by international war, civil war and their consequences in the first half of the twentieth century: the First World War, the Russian Revolution, the Spanish Civil War, the Easter Rising, the Second World War, the war in the Pacific, and the Communist Revolution of China. These events shaped the political consciousness of different generations and determined their objective possibilities. As the research of Glen Elder (1974) has shown, the generation that came to maturity in the 1930s had to confront a set of circumstances that were especially problematic in terms of the sequence of events from the First World War, the Depression and the rise of fascism.

However, the direct experience of war was not significant in the formation of the generation of people born in the immediate post-1945 period. This cohort grew up in a completely different social environment. Unlike their fathers and grandfathers, men from this cohort did not have to submit to military conscription and they had no significant experience of threat or armed combat. Crises in Suez, Aden, the Malaysian peninsula, Rhodesia, Kenya and the Malvinas islands were typically short and remote. Harold Macmillan's 'winds of change' speech about political change in Africa and the policy of gradual withdrawal from imperial rule prevented Britain from being dragged into expensive colonial wars. The United States, Portugal, Belgium and France were all drawn into 'hot' wars that proved to be painful, expensive and damaging to democracy. Imperial wars were increasingly difficult because subject peoples were themselves mobilized against imperial subjection. In retrospect, the view that the 'British, more by luck than good management, had perceived this truth in time and retired from the business of empire with comparative ease and dignity' (Brogan 1985: 672) is entirely plausible. It was also the era of the rise of cultural consumerism. One of the ways the Conservatives had beaten Labour was by the celebration of consumerism ushered in by getting rid of wartime economy standards and expressed in the election slogan 'Bonfire of Controls' and Macmillan's declaration that 'You've never had it so good.'

While the post-war period was a persistent illustration of the 'British disease' in economic terms, the sixties generation was strategic in aesthetic, cultural and sexual terms. The post-war baby boomers were the first generation to live through a time when a mass consumer revolution transformed popular taste and lifestyles. It involved a 'cultural revolution' that was driven by an entrepreneurial spirit and involved the creation of new subcultures in opposition to established society; the growth of individualism, consumerism and entrepreneurialism; the creation of a youth culture; the development of new technologies (television, long-playing records, transistor radios, refrigerators, jet travel and the contraceptive pill); the spread of television and the spectacle into everyday life; the globalization of cultural exchange, especially pop and mass cultures; massive improvements in the material quality of life; the growth of permissiveness in conjunction with major disruptions to traditional social relationships in terms of class, family and ethnicity (Marwick 1998: 17–18). New possibilities in self-expression and the promotion of a participatory popular culture were channelled through rock music and rock festivals. The rise of popular culture and its penetration of high culture was seen by many social scientists as the decline of the authority of the intellectual and a written culture. The decline of grand narratives was eventually hailed as the origins of postmodernity (Rojek and Turner 1998).

The post-war transformation of British society involved significant antagonism between classes over cultural identity. The literary and film successes of the 1960s were characteristically concerned with the entry of working-class and popular culture into national consciousness. In this respect, the British 'New Wave' of the late 1950s and early 1960s celebrated the aggressive and problematic working-class hero on the verge of breaking into middle-class life in such works as *The Loneliness of the Long Distance Runner*, *Saturday Night and Sunday Morning*, *Room at the Top*, *Look Back in Anger*, *Alfie*, *This Sporting Life* and *Billy Liar*. Such cultural products were important signs of an influential generation of British writers and yet the passivity of post-war British generations is also reflected in the literary output of its high culture.

These changes as a whole were related to the arrival of a youth culture and what Talcott Parsons in 'Religion in postindustrial America' called the 'expressive revolution' (Parsons 1999: 16). The social changes of the time were important in creating the conditions for the emergence of a strategic generation: a dramatic shift in the demographic structure of post-war Britain; an adversarial relationship to previous ('square') generations; and the creation of cultural leaders, spaces and events to celebrate the sixties generation. While the post-war generation watched Britain slowly but surely decline as a world power, they also experienced a degree of cultural leadership within the new youth culture through the global success of British pop groups especially the Beatles and the Stones. Despite the importance of American developments in popular culture, there was an association between national identity and popular culture. British popular culture enjoyed a particularly high status in the late 1960s and was especially influential internationally. That Britain was at the vanguard of this trend was evident in the press coverage of the time that used concepts such as 'the British years' and 'swinging London' (Marwick 1998: 455–6).

Earlier generations saw this cultural revolution as a betrayal of British culture. Being a successful generation in terms of orchestrating a revolution in popular culture has also been seen as an abdication of political responsibility by an older generation. For intellectuals such as Richard Hoggart and Raymond Williams, the spread of post-war popular culture destroyed the basic communal dimension of British socialism. In *The Way We Live Now* Hoggart (1995) provides a sustained critique of some of the consequences of the transformations that have taken place in the post-war period. In particular, he suggests that one of the legacies of the 1960s cultural shifts is a resort to relativism in a variety of spheres, but especially in culture and education. He is critical also of the concentration on youth and the pleasure industry as well as unreflecting uses of concepts of multiculturalism, which have, to his mind, stunted intellectual enquiry.

The rise of sixties culture also led, in some quarters, to a nostalgia for the past and a sense of loss over the disappearance of culture, especially rural and religious culture. John Betjeman's celebration of suburban England, of tennis clubs and railway stations, offered a testimony to the disappearance of traditional patterns of middle-class life. Philip Larkin's world was also a struggle to come to terms with his inner life and the norms of English provincial society in the 1950s. His distaste for sixties culture pervaded his poetry and he deplored the permissiveness that he thought started in this period, complaining that 'sexual intercourse began in 1963'. Later, the authoritarian strand of New Right thinkers associated with journals such as the *Salisbury Review* similarly lamented the passing of traditional English culture through multiculturalism as well as traditional family and personal values (see Levitas 1986).

In *The Uses of Literacy* (Hoggart 1958) and *Culture and Society* (Williams 1958) there is a nostalgic cultural theory from an earlier generation of academics who saw the decline of working-class communities as eroding the social roots of socialism. Raymond Williams (1921–88), an important figure in the transition of English literary theory to cultural studies, struggled to establish a critical theory of British history (Williams 1989). However, there is a general agreement that post-war Britain failed to produce any social scientist of any international stature. It is plausible to suggest that the communal dimension of English class consciousness, documented by historians like Eric Hobsbawm and E. P. Thompson, came to an end under the Thatcher government with the miners' strike. This conflict was not only the end of mining as a significant industry but the termination of a style of communal life and politics as documented in sociological studies such as *Coal is Our Life* (Dennis *et al.* 1962). With the fragmentation of social class as the pivotal feature of English social structure, alternative forms of political and social consciousness have emerged such as gender and generational consciousness.

If generation as a principle of social division is closely related to the status order, then it is possible to suggest that one aspect of Weber's view of the history of social stratification has been vindicated. The erosion of class identity has been replaced by status and status politics, within which generational alliances have become increasingly important. There is some evidence of an oscillation of active and passive generations in British history: an active wartime generation, a passive inter-war generation, an active consumer generation, and a passive generation X. As the baby boomer generation came to dominate the labour market and the new leisure industries, it created conditions that prevented the rise of an alternative strategic generation. Those who followed the sixties generation were forced to be generation X. The sixties generation had set up the liberal institutions and so the next generation had very little to do. The adventure had been taken away from them. Generation X accepted the cultural and political heritage of their parents' generation because their protest vehicle had been taken over. They have been described (Lopez 2002) as the 'heroes of silence' 'fleeing from the disorder of the generation' that gave them what they got but also caused their problems: social inequality, public insecurity and lack of solidarity.

America and *The Closing of the American Mind*

The pessimistic take on the impact of the 1960s on contemporary culture has also been applied to America. There has been a whole swathe of writings that, while sympathetic to some of the liberal reforms of the era, have suggested that the predominant effects of the sixties have been negative. This view can be found in Allen J. Matusow's *The Unravelling of America* (1984); W. L. O'Neill's *Coming Apart* (1971); John M. Blum's *Years of Discord* (1991) and David Burner's *Making Peace With the 60s* (1996). And in *Destructive Generation* Peter Collier and David Horowitz maintained that sixties developments turned American society into a 'collection of splinter groups' (Marwick 1998: 9).

However, it was *The Closing of the American Mind* (1987) by Allan Bloom that provided one of the most influential critiques of the 1960s generation. It continues to be the starting point of current debates that seek to go beyond polemical reactions to it (Buckley and Seaton 1992). The study is a classic example of the high water mark of the conservative response to the legacy of the cultural changes that have their roots in the 1960s. In it Bloom explored the social and political consequences of the cultural changes orchestrated by radical students through the medium of the institutions of higher education in America. He maintained that the result of the changes wrought by these discontented post-war students has been overwhelmingly negative, failing American democracy and impoverishing the cultural lives of modern students. His thesis, which implicitly develops a theory of generational change, is both complex and sophisticated. It has therefore been a worthy target of social criticism.

Bloom's (1987) analysis of the closure of the American ideal starts with the argument that the affluent and comfortable generations of post-war students did not have any personal experience of the struggles and deprivations of their parents. They did not have the exhilaration of social mobility that many migrant groups from war-torn Europe had encountered as a consequence of settlement in America. For earlier generations, the American dream was often a reality involving both a rags to riches trajectory and a genuine appreciation of the democratic opportunities of post-war America. According to Bloom, the affluent students of the sixties were a pampered generation that took for granted the legacy of the American constitution and the values of the founding fathers. Indeed, they were often antagonistic towards this version of liberal democracy. The sixties students were offered a diet of cultural relativism and Marxism that regarded the Constitution as a historically specific text and moreover the product of the interest of private property. Consequently, there has been an impoverishment of education as a civilizing process and a translation of 'education' into merely technical instruction. Bloom therefore felt that the post-war generation is poorly equipped to offer any convincing or authoritative moral education to its children, and this loss of vision has occurred in a context where the family itself is clearly under stress.

Bloom illustrates this thesis by suggesting that the affluent generations of the post-war period have lost any interest in or understanding of the culture of books. They are a generation singularly lacking any educated view of the canon of western literature:

> Though students do not have books, they most emphatically do have music. Nothing is more singular about this generation than its addiction to music. This is the age of music and the states of soul that accompany it.
>
> (Bloom 1987: 68)

Of course, this 'music' is largely limited to rock music and Bloom notes that his students are generally speaking totally ignorant about classical music. He sees their musical habitus as both shallow and narrow and believes that rock music, which has risen on the ashes of classical music, does not offer any education in the sense of regulating passion in the interests of the cultivation of the spirit, but rather celebrates raw sexuality. Everyday life has been colonized by commercial interests that manipulate the sexual appetite of the young in the overt pursuit of profit. Popular culture is in some respects the product of the sixties and combines sex and the capitalist economy. Its representative figure has been Mick Jagger (Bloom 1987: 78). Although Bloom's text may sound like a religious objection to sex, drugs and rock and roll, his main anxiety is about the educational consequences of popular culture, namely the impoverishment of the soul.

There are good reasons for reading *The Closing of the American Mind* as a contemporary commentary on Alexis de Tocqueville's reflections on American political culture in 1835 and 1840. In *Democracy in America*, Tocqueville (1945) outlined two basic fears for the new nation. The first was the impact of the radical doctrine of egalitarianism on independent thought, because he assumed that a mass democracy would exterminate private conscience and individual creativity. The second was a fear of material abundance within which self-interest would stand in the way of public duty. A culture of possessive individualism would be incompatible with public responsibility (MacPherson 1962). This fear that hedonism would corrupt the new democracy was shared by Thomas Jefferson (Koch and Peden 1944: 139) who wrote in 1787 that 'a rich country cannot long be a free one'. Jefferson and Tocqueville were in fact dependent on classical literature that in its analysis of the crisis of the Roman world had lamented the growth of hedonism and self-interest. Tocqueville followed Tacitus in his view that the foundations of any empire were corrupted by wealth and that a successful social system required discipline and asceticism (Boesche 1988).

Bloom's fears for modern America run along similar lines. Affluence and comfort have produced a youth generation that is condemned to mediocrity. The growth of mass culture has robbed youth of the sentiments and training that are necessary to appreciate serious culture. The American mind is closed by its very success. There is an irony of which Bloom would disapprove. The postmodern social theorist Jean Baudrillard (1988: 97), reflecting on Tocqueville, noted in his *America* that

> Everything that has been played out and destroyed in Europe in the name of Revolution and Terror has been realised in its simplest, most

empirical form on the other side of the Atlantic (the utopia of wealth, rights, freedom, the social contract, and representation).

Like Tocqueville, Bloom believes that the radical doctrine of individual equality produces a shallow world in which social conflict is avoided. Individuals are allowed to believe what they like, provided it is sufficiently banal not to cause offence. Egalitarianism has not, however, brought more freedom to the lives of the modern generation. The sexual revolution that was explored under the banner of individual freedom produced only boredom. The feminist revolution that marched under the banner of equality only resulted in dissatisfaction with familial and personal relationships as sexuality and commercialism joined forces. Feminist criticism of the commercialization of sex in industrial capitalism merged with right-wing Christian criticism of modern society. Of course, evangelical Christians are often openly critical of feminism, but they implicitly converge in their attitudes towards sexual exploitation and the negative effects of divorce on children (Smith 2000: 162–5).

Again Bloom follows Tocqueville on the family in American democracy. For Tocqueville, the generation that created the American Revolution destroyed the aristocratic family. In a democracy, family relations become more affectionate and egalitarian, and the authority of the father is diminished. The family was no longer able to inculcate an ethic of public duty, because the notion of the family and society as stable and enduring social institutions that create definite obligations is obscured. Hence the family cannot contain destructive self-interest in an affluent society. Sexual liberation not only released women from traditional roles and assumptions, but it also liberated men from the conventional roles of parenthood and breadwinner. Now women are presented with the combined burdens of reproduction and employment. As a result, 'the promise of modernity is not really fulfilled for women' (Bloom 1987: 114). This failure of the sexual revolution to produce a satisfactory gender balance was also a central feature of *Love and Friendship* (Bloom 1993: 117) where Bloom, reflecting on Rousseau's views of marriage, argued that contemporary society has provided women with neither freedom nor equality. In fact the incompatibility of individual freedom and social equality was a theme in Tocqueville's political philosophy that is highly congenial to Bloom's general purpose (Bloom 1987: 98).

In his reflections on the social and cultural consequences of the sixties revolution, Bloom, as we have seen, derives support from Tocqueville's reflections on nineteenth-century America. However, he is most critical of the sociological writings that sprang from the post-war generational revolution. For Bloom, the great legacy of Continental philosophy, or what he calls 'the German connection' (Bloom 1987: 141–56), has been trivialized and Americanized by the post-war generation. This criticism includes sociology where the critical legacy of Max Weber's social science has been 'routinised' (Bloom 1987: 151) by Talcott Parsons, who has converted the cultural pathos of Weber's vision of capitalism into banality.

A similar criticism is brought against Herbert Marcuse, whose critical theory played a large role in the development of the sixties consciousness. According to Bloom Marcuse betrayed the German legacy. While Marcuse started as a serious Hegel scholar, 'he ended up here writing trashy culture criticism with a heavy sex interest in *One Dimensional Man* and other well known books' (Bloom 1987: 226). For Bloom, the great inspiration of culture in the last two hundred years has come, not from people inspired by the traditions of the Left, socialism and humanism, but from 'men of the Right; and Nietzsche is in that respect merely their complement' (Bloom 1987: 223). The German connection is a betrayal and a farce, because the Left has attempted to embrace and domesticate the traditions of the Right through Nietzsche, Heidegger, Weber and more recently Carl Schmitt.

Commentators have also drawn parallels between Bloom and Leo Strauss. For example, in *Leo Strauss and the American Right* Shadia Drury (1997: 111) has claimed that Bloom's criticism of the American mind 'is the most successful popularisation and application of Strauss's ideas to America'. Both Strauss and Bloom regard liberalism as a major threat to an authentic culture and politics. Strauss in particular has detected a parallel between the Weimar Republic that prepared the way towards German fascism and the liberalism of the United States that will descend into relativism, nihilism and emptiness. He defined the sixties as 'the period of dogmatic answers and trivial tracts' and argued that sixties intellectuals were as destructive as the Nazis (Marwick 1998: 4).

In summary, Bloom has condemned American culture because its possessive individualism cannot constrain self-interest and therefore a public culture is not possible. Bloom also argues that American pluralism and the melting pot society will paradoxically only encourage inter-ethnic violence and rivalry; no love of country can emerge from a mixture of individualism, commercialism and multicultural politics. In any case, the ideals of liberalism are a thin disguise for the dominance of commercial interests. The neo-conservative platform of Strauss and Bloom argues that passion for America, as established by the founding fathers and the Constitution, cannot be sustained in a climate of individualism and relativism. Patriotic passion is eroded by the sexual foundations of popular and commercial culture. Love of country is denied the post-war generation, because they cannot grasp the forms of political life.

The actual generation of the sixties is rapidly becoming part of American history rather than a contemporary reality. Bloom (1987: 333) is cynical about the people who were part of the sixties generation:

> What remains is a certain self-promotion by people who took part in it all, now in their forties, having come to terms with the 'establishment' but dispersing a nostalgic essence in the media, where, of course, many of them are flourishing, admitting that it was unreal but asserting that it was the moment of significance.

Bloom argues that the real progress in race relations, in the democratization of education, and in changes in the public status of women took place outside the universities and in the community, but that these changes are often falsely claimed by the radical student generation.

The dominant mood of Bloom's criticism is one of nostalgia. This neo-conservative thought can be understood as nostalgia for the national consciousness of the founding fathers. Reich (1970) distinguished between three different types of American consciousness. The first, expressing the formation of a new nation, was highly individualistic and focused on the rewards of hard work. It was an expression of the original American dream that envisaged a community based on individual dignity. In the post-Second World War period, this gave way to a new consciousness which, responding to the failures of excessive individualism and inequality, stressed the importance of organization and rational hierarchy of authority where the individual worked for the common good. The new American consciousness that emerged in the 1960s overturned both extreme individualism and rationality. It developed out of the tensions that arose because of the contradiction between the promise made to young Americans through affluence, new technology and so on and the threat to that promise posed by boring jobs, the Vietnam war and the threat of nuclear war (Reich 1970: 184).

For Bloom, modern America has not remained faithful to the radical vision of the generation of the founding fathers. The sixties generation are condemned, because they are almost wholly alienated from the world of Jeffersonian democracy. The founding fathers found their inspiration in a classical vision of the republic and the city. The self-interest of the sixties is a fundamental departure from the foundation values of service in the public arena. It is also possible to see Bloom's critique of American education, for example in his dismissal of new trends in the curriculum such as women's studies, as reflecting a more deeply-rooted tradition of opposition to the 'public woman' and a conservative defence of traditional values in men/women relations (Jones 1989).

Bloom's critical attack on American liberalism is powerful and comprehensive. Whether his position is correct is less central here than the way his work is interesting because it attributes considerable social importance to generational experiences. However, it is not possible entirely to ignore Bloom's actual claims, because they do have a close relationship to our own argument about the cultural significance of the 1960s. It is interesting to note that many liberals and radicals would agree with Bloom's analysis of American commercial culture. Indeed, his understanding of the decline in patriotic commitment to public politics is not dissimilar to the defence of patriotic sentiment in Richard Rorty's *Achieving Our Country* (1998). Bloom's critique of American liberalism would receive some support within the liberal camp. Whereas those on the right regret the supposed collapse of traditional cultural heritages, those on the extreme left tend to be equally critical, suggesting that the counter-cultural practices were simply exploited by commercial interests and there was no redistribution of economic or social power. On the soft left too, it is commonly thought that although the decade was exciting, it left no long-lasting legacy (Marwick 1998: 4). Moreover, a lot of the criticism of the 1960s has also come from feminists and minorities who felt they had been marginalized by the events of the time.

There are other issues that put a question mark on the historical accuracy of Bloom's account. One obvious point to note is that, if the sixties culture produced a liberal or left-wing component, it is also the case that there was a right-wing student lobby. In this respect, the sixties university lobby was an extremely heterogeneous social movement. Thus in America, while there was widespread left-wing protest, there was simultaneously a wave of protest among youth on the right. Organizations such as 'Young Americans for Freedom', a youth organization founded in 1960 at the estate of William F. Buckle, provided the source of contemporary conservatism. For youth on the right the 1960s represented the decade of 'an important battle against communism' and a pathbreaking book, *The Conscience of a Conservative* by Barry Goldwater (Klatch 1999: 1). Moreover, there is a strong polemical current running through the thesis and the claims made in it seem to rest on rather thin ice, being based largely on Bloom's personal impressions of developments in a small number of universities.

In terms of our interests, one of the weakest aspects of Bloom's thesis is that it completely ignores the impact of Korea and Vietnam on the experience of generations of young Americans, who had missed the Second

World War. Bloom's argument is that American post-war generations do not understand the American dream because they were products of peaceful affluence. However, the Vietnam war was central in creating the consciousness of young Americans. It was the insecurity generated by this war together with the threat of nuclear annihilation that sharpened the views of the 1960s generation and brought them together in reaction against their parents' experiences (Reich 1970: 186–7). Young Americans were genuinely traumatized by this war; moreover, it was completely unlike the Second World War because it had a damaging and corrosive impact on American national identity.

There are other historical problems with Bloom's position. The implication of Bloom's argument is that the utopian dream of student radicalism actually changed western society. One can certainly identify changes in culture and values, but many aspects of economics and politics were not transformed. One could argue that many of the policy implications and objectives of the liberal phase of post-war reconstruction were defeated or curtailed by the ideological currents that Bloom represents. While we want to argue that the culture of the second half of the twentieth century was shaped by the sixties, many substantive aspects of that period were destroyed by the neo-conservative reaction in the forms of Reagan and Thatcher administrations. The ambition to create egalitarian systems of education and health was abandoned in the late 1970s as western governments turned to deregulation and privatization as solutions to the growing tax burden. Similarly, both the Reagan and Bush administrations pursued exactly the sort of social conservatism advocated by Bloom in a whole range of spheres, including education (Jones 1992: 68). In Britain, one reason for (re)introducing market forces into (especially higher) education as well as saving public money was to narrow down students' focus on to getting a good degree, good job, high income – forgetting about any wider social or political campaigning.

Moreover, the views of Bloom and Strauss had a profound effect on the ideological reorganization of the Republican Party. The conservative wing of American politics is Straussian and regarded Bill Clinton's brand of democratic politics as itself a legacy of the sixties; hence the debates surrounding Clinton's postgraduate studies during the late 1960s which meant that he avoided the Vietnam draft. 'New Right' economists sympathetic to Bloom suggest that Kennedy's/Johnson's peacetime 'War on Poverty' – via (for Americans) more generous welfare benefits alongside a full employment policy – also undermined American character by creating dependency culture in place of the founding fathers' self-help. Reagan, who as Californian governor repressed rioting students in the later 1960s, started to dismantle the welfare state and union rights in the 1980s. In Britain, under Thatcherism, as well as the free market ideology, there was a new emphasis on the importance of traditional family values and an explicit denigration of sixties theories which Thatcher herself described as 'permissive claptrap' (Marwick 1998: 4).

Conclusion: balancing the impact of the 1960s

Critics of sixties culture think that it somehow destroyed the national character of the various countries that fell victim to it. There is a general view that this period ushered in a cultural relativism that pervaded all aspects of social life, rendering meaningless the idea of standards rooted in any traditional sense. Popular culture has undermined the inherent superiority of high culture. There is also a sense that the rise of multiculturalism has sharpened inter-ethnic conflict and that the new roles for women have presented more problems than solutions; that the permissiveness in personal relations has led to the breakdown of the traditional family to detrimental effect. Thus in the UK there is a view that the events of this decade had a detrimental effect on the traditional values of the English nation in particular. And in America, it is thought that the sixties has damaged the cultural heritage established by the founding fathers and undermined the public spirit of that nation, principally through changes in the education system.

However, we would argue that the most far-reaching changes were more visible in the cultural and intellectual spheres and that these were generally positive. The intellectual climate produced by the 1960s was not as impoverished as suggested by critics of the era. Sixties intellectuals were more 'classless' than previously. They were often the products of grammar schools in the UK and affirmative action in the US. They used Marxism as a theoretical base for radicalism but quickly saw its limitations and took issue with the intellectual Marxists who espoused it but did nothing practical with it. For example, in France Sartre shifted ground to a more practical application of ideas in his departure from the classic intellectual to the new intellectual who, he thought, should become integrated with the masses to achieve real social changes (De Beauvoir 1984: 4). Moreover, the Frankfurt School ran into problems by not going for such 'praxis' as shown in the *New Left Review*'s Marcuse–Adorno exchange (January/February 1999: 118–36). The turmoil of the 1960s, far from weakening intellectual output, was especially fertile for the development of new paradigms in social thought and for influencing the shape of new social movements.

There seems therefore to be a need for a more cautious approach to assessing the impact of this decade. Marwick (1998: 17–20) has suggested that the concept of 'measured judgement' could best capture the most interesting developments in the sixties, which he sees as a genuine liberal tolerance of diversity and willingness to accommodate new subcultures. It was members of the elite who exercised this measured judgement in their response to or anticipation of the claims of protest groups that was critical to the social welfare advances that characterized the post-war period. In particular, he suggests that there is reason to believe that generalized tolerance for multiculturalism has become rooted (despite certain exceptions) and that this stemmed from the ideals that were first expressed in the 1960s. Although there are manifestly examples of racism, multiculturalism (and its celebration) may well prove to be the most important legacy of the cultural revolution. In Britain at least, the lack of tolerance for racism is what forced people such as Norman Tebbit and other post-Powell figures in the early twenty-first century to attack multiculturalism because they realize it is politically unacceptable to attack multi-racialism.

Moreover, although it may be that high cultural forms are now being taken over by more popular forms of cultural expression, this development is not necessarily superficial. Bloom's distaste for rock music ignores the fact that the roots of rock and roll went a long way back – to black musicians of the early twentieth century who were themselves carrying on a tradition. White musicians developing this music in the sixties were aware of and acknowledged their debt to the previous generations and the traditions they were drawing on. Many blues singers would not have got the public recognition they deserved if it had not been for the way groups like the Rolling Stones acknowledged their input. Janis Joplin, for example, was central to the reinvention of the blues in a multicultural environment and carriers of black musical traditions into mainstream American culture (Eyerman and Jamison 2000: 132–3). Although the sixties bands could be accused of stealing black music it was not resented because, first, they acknowledged the heritage and second, because of discrimination blacks could not get into the music industry. It could therefore be argued that middle-class white trailblazers were important because they put black music into the market and then opened up a route by which black musicians themselves could enter. For example, John Coltrane appearing with the Rolling Stones (whose name came from one of his songs); the Beatles with Ravi Shankar; Muddy Waters putting his catalogue on record at an age of over 60.

In terms of the economy, there is more ambivalence. On many basic questions relating to the economy there seems to have been a shift in the direction advocated by Bloom. Some of this trend has been captured in the McDonaldization thesis; namely that things become trivialized because they are generalized. Here it is suggested that there has been a significant movement towards casualized, exploited labour serving up inferior consumer products. Richard Sennett (1998) has also pointed up the negative side effects of economic trends. While there is clear evidence to support this position, there are some legacies offered by the sixties generation that run in the opposite direction. It is possible to suggest that the era gave rise to a whole new generation of what could be described as 'enlightened entrepreneurialism'. Figures such as Richard Branson, Anita Roddick and Alan Sugar captured the spirit of the sixties in their enterprises. Branson started in the record industry; Sugar's first venture was selling stereos and Roddick ventured into sustainable trade and environmentalism. On the one hand these people had the idealism of the time, showing that society can be different. On the other hand, they showed that life could not be all about hippiedom.

These people wanted to react against social orthodoxy but, having seen the unworkable side of the 1960s, also wanted to engage in ventures that were economically valid. People such as these, even if professional jobs had been available to them, would have resisted the constraints of their parents' generation's orthodoxy. On the production side they support stronger workers' rights, for example, part-timers getting full-time privileges, minimum wage and Social Charter being accepted and third world sweatshops being avoided. On the consumption side, they offer products that were not only open to an elite, for example, transatlantic flights, cheap flexible mortgages, cheap hi-fi. The US also has its Branson-type figures such as Ted Turner providing 24-hour news and donating to the UN/charities; Robert Waterman with his 'green' power company (and his ex-colleague Tom Peters advocating 'hippie' management styles). And then there is Steve Case of America On Line (AOL) getting people online.

Finally, the view that the sixties generation is a selfish 'we' generation is not necessarily well founded. Recent research has shown that members of this generation today still show a high level of social conscience and commitment. This is mainly expressed in their concerns about environmental issues, population growth, economic rationalism and selfish materialism as well as the continuation of social inequalities (Riggs and Turner 2000). This finding ties in with some of the arguments made by Robert D. Putnam (2000) about social capital and civic engagement. Putnam has suggested that there has been a general downwards trend in social capital (networks, norms and trust that inspire cooperation within communities). That is, that social capital was highest among people who lived during the wars and lowest among the contemporary young generation. Nevertheless, although according to this schema people born in the immediate post-war period have less social capital than the preceding generation, they remain tolerant and accepting of diversity. Moreover, people who are starting to retire now are beginning to reinvolve themselves in the community. It is therefore arguable whether the political trends that started under Thatcherism and Reaganism have undermined the activism of the sixties generation. There is evidence that it is still this generation rather than their offspring that is continuing to be involved in protest. It therefore seems plausible to suggest that you get an active generation that builds up social capital because it is socially engaged which is followed by a generation that just uses up the social capital structures put in place by previous generations.

The radical legacy of the peace movement can be seen today in Greenpeace, in environmental lobbies, in attitudes towards migration, race and pluralism, and in attempts to challenge some of the more negative aspects of globalization. While it is true that some of the movements of the time were led by white, middle-class men and some of the practices were explicitly sexist, it remains the case that the period was critical to later institutions and practices that paved the way for women's rights and minority rights.

CHAPTER 3

Generations, intellectuals and social movements

Traditional sociological perspectives have typically seen class as important to the formation of intellectual traditions. This approach, for example, was characteristic of Antonio Gramsci's (1971) thinking and later of Bourdieu (1988) who saw intellectuals as a subordinate stratum in the dominant class. In contrast, Mannheim (1997b) defined independent intellectuals as 'free floating'. What he meant by this was that intellectuals were not a class in any Marxist sense, nor were they attached to any particular class or political party. He argued that intellectual activity was free from the constraints imposed by belonging to a particular socially defined class and that intellectuals were drawn from a variety of different strata. Intellectuals were not shaped by specific economic interests. Thus, their distance from any particular class position meant that they were unfettered by vested interests and were therefore in a position to carry out independent enquiry into social processes (Turner 1999: 119–20).

An important theme in this book is that of the relationship between generations and intellectuals. Collins's (1998) exploration of the development of philosophies has been almost unique in addressing the relationship between generations and major intellectual trends in sociology.

Sociology's traditional neglect of this area has not been replicated in other disciplines, especially those looking at intellectual trends in America. For example, in *America and the Young Intellectual* Stearns (1921) coined the term 'lost generation' to describe young scholars who had left America for Europe in the belief that Europe offered a more interesting intellectual (and less commercially driven) climate. And in *The Last Intellectuals* Jacoby (1987) has claimed that intellectual generations of the type that existed in 1950s and 1960s America have disappeared; the 'public' intellectual has been replaced by privatized, career-oriented academics. Michael Ignatieff (1997) has made a comparable argument about western Europe, suggesting that along with the increased access to education there has been a decline in the independent, public intellectual.

In this chapter, we explore the topic of 'strategic' intellectual generations through a number of case studies, drawing on some of the ideas inspired by Bourdieu and Mannheim. This theme takes us back to Mannheim's ([1936] 1997b) paradigm in *Ideology and Utopia*. For Mannheim, utopia is understood as a set of ideas that push in the direction of changing the status quo whereas nostalgia involves ideas that push activities towards preserving the status quo. We argue that intellectuals (analogous to rising and falling classes) are important in articulating either utopian (forward looking) or ideological (backward looking) visions. Mannheim's book on *Conservatism* ([1986] 1997c) was a particularly important version of this theory. Here he considered how various forms of conservatism were related to different patterns of intellectual life and to different social circumstances. We suggest further that utopian and nostalgic generations might alternate historically.

In the following pages we look at these issues through a range of more detailed discussions of generations of intellectual elites in America and France. This will involve a discussion of the impact of historical dislocations (recognized by Mannheim himself) in the forging of intellectual generations through a consideration of the disruption of late twentieth-century generations of migrant intellectuals, including the Frankfurt School, the New York Intellectuals (who are a classic example of generational and ethnic consciousness) and diasporic intellectuals such as Edward Said. Finally, it will consider generational shifts in French intellectual life, looking particularly at figures such as Jean-Paul Sartre, Simone de Beauvoir and Michel Foucault.

We want to underline the importance of major traumatic events in shaping intellectual trends, that is, fascism, war, depression, exile and migration. In typological terms, we suggest that the collapse of a nation (Poland, the Soviet Union, occupied France) produces nostalgic, tragic or melancholic visions of national crisis. Thus, for example, the existential philosophies of 1930s and 1940s (early Sartre and Heidegger) were expressions of European collapse. We stress generational changes in relation to the Depression (in America), the Second World War (which forced intellectuals to confront Stalinism and fascism making them become more supportive of America as a democracy); the Cold War and McCarthyism and the end of intellectual realism through postmodernism, an intellectual trend that stressed chaos in the context of stability and certainty. However, following Bourdieu's thinking on generational conflict, we also want to show how younger generations of intellectuals are forced to challenge the hegemony of their predecessors if they are to make an impact in the competitive field of intellectuals. In order to make their mark, they need to borrow from previous generations' heritages but also to challenge and overturn them. Ultimately this chapter aims to show that intellectual generations in a state of homelessness create an impulse towards thinking seriously about national identity, diasporic membership and cosmopolitanism.

Intellectual generations and migration

As Kumar (1993) has shown, there has been a strong current of anti-utopianism running through the thought of intellectual émigrés (in particular from the Soviet Union or Austria and Germany during the Second World War) who felt they had suffered from the utopian politics of their original countries. These émigrés often launched their attacks on the utopian traditions that shaped their previous experiences while in exile in countries such as America, France or Britain. This protest might well be expressed through novels, as was the case in Yevgeny Zamyatin's *We* ([1934] 1993). Exiled to France, Zamyatin produced a sharp satire on the Soviet Union. However, it was Arthur Koestler's *Darkness at Noon* (1940), a dark condemnation of Soviet communism, that was the most well known of these anti-utopian novels.

As well as novelists, various exiled social and political theorists also produced works that were anti-utopian. For example, having emigrated to New Zealand, Karl Popper wrote *The Open Society and Its Enemies* ([1945] 1995) directly in response to the Nazi invasion of Austria. Openly condemning both fascism and Marxism as sharing general theories of history and adhering to a predetermined view of historical change, this book remains one of the most influential critiques of utopianism. Another exile from Austria, Friedrich von Hayek, published *The Road to Serfdom*

([1944] 1980), a book that similarly drew parallels between fascism and communism portraying both as extreme manifestations of collectivism. As an exile first in Britain and later Israel, Jacob Talmon wrote *The Origins of Totalitarian Democracy* (1952) in which he argued that modern totalitarianism stemmed directly from eighteenth-century French utopian thought. Finally, the Polish dissident Leszek Kolakowski provided a sustained critique of utopian ideas and focused his attack specifically on Marxism which he saw as a particularly destructive form of totalitarianism (Kumar 1993: 65–7).

Isaiah Berlin provides a further example of this trend. Berlin visited Russia in the 1930s and saw how it was starving the peasants and imprisoning intellectual dissidents. His meeting in 1945 with the dissident poet Anna Akhmatova led to her long persecution by Stalin and his successors. Deeply affected by these events, Berlin adopted an anticommunist stand, suggesting that its determinism denied pluralism, which he saw as integral to a liberal system because people have contradictory beliefs and desires. Moreover, he thought its utopianism demanded self-sacrifice on the part of people for some supposed future (Ignatieff 2000).

Drawing on Mannheim's thinking on intellectuals, the Frankfurt School is a good example of a nostalgic intellectual generation shaped by the experience of migration and exile. The school itself consisted of two generations with Max Horkheimer, Theodor Adorno, Herbert Marcuse, Friedrich Pollock, Franz Neumann, Leo Lowenthal and Erich Fromm being central to the first generation of the Frankfurt School. Most of the early members of the Frankfurt School were born around the turn of the nineteenth century and almost all of them came from upper-class and middle-class backgrounds, coming together through the Institute of Social Research founded in 1924 in Germany (Jay 1973). Jürgen Habermas was the central thinker of the second generation, distinguishing himself from his mentors by rejecting some of the central threads of their thinking, especially the anti-Enlightenment current.

The intellectual thought of the Frankfurt School was produced in reaction to the variety of historical developments that occurred throughout the production of their works. Their intellectual product spanned the First World War; the revolution in Russia; the Depression; fascism and the Cold War. All of these traumatic events, perhaps especially Stalinism and fascism, undermined reductionist approaches to history and demanded a reinvention of traditional Marxist theory. The critical theorists were decisive to the creation of a new idea of western Marxism, a concept that was itself associated with the 1950s and with theorists whose intellectual development was consolidated in the post-Second World War period

(Therborn 1998: 58–63). This range of historical events thus provided the backdrop to the development of critical theory: the Frankfurt School was instrumental in producing a critical paradigm shift in intellectual Marxism and the rejuvenation of this tradition of thought in western Europe and America. Although their outlook was rooted in the classic political economy perspective and they clearly drew on and benefited from an intellectual heritage that included Marxism, German idealism and psychoanalysis, they forged a distinctive identity by distinguishing themselves from these traditions (Jay 1973: 43).

Social movements and what we can call 'movement intellectuals' play an essential role in challenging and overturning dominant intellectual paradigms. The essential aspect of social movements and their intellectuals is their role in the formation of collective identity. Under certain circumstances, social movements can become vehicles for the emergence of generational consciousness and conflict and vice versa. That is, generational experiences can provide a root for the emergence of collective identity, social movements and, subsequently, for generational conflict.

The Frankfurt School's influence on the 1960s generation was particularly significant. Their opposition to nationalist violence and their emphasis on cultural and personal politics informed the intellectual protest movements of this decade and became especially influential in America and Germany. It could thus be argued that this group of intellectuals pre-empted the new social movements' emphasis on personal politics (Calhoun 1998: 450–1). Herbert Marcuse in particular came to be seen as the 'star' of this decade of intellectual protest with his arguments about repression and commoditization. *Eros and Civilization* ([1955] 1987) was formative to the development of 1960s sub-cultures. Here he offered a wide-ranging critique of modern society, presenting it as repressive and obsessed with productivity and power and drawing parallels between the United States and the Soviet Union. He was politically active in issues such as the Cuban missile crisis and Vietnam, relentlessly contesting American justification for their actions and describing the US as a totalitarian democracy (Marwick 1998: 291–2).

It was during this decade, moreover, that the Frankfurt School's ideas became more widely accessible through the diffusion of a number of their earlier works in western Europe and their publication in English (Jay 1986: 95–6). Key concepts introduced by these critical theorists were picked up by the New Left and introduced into their journals. These German refugees were the source from which the left began to discuss racism, imperialism and oppression and to oppose the rationality of modern America, and concepts such as 'alienation', 'reification' and 'negation' started to litter the language of the left-wing literature (Diggins 1994: 404).

However, despite the potential for political activism, the overriding mood of the Frankfurt School's intellectual output was pessimistic and nostalgic. The main thrust of their critique of America was to condemn the country's intellectual heritage as a manifestation of scientific control, to suggest that the idea of progress was just an illusion and that technology, consumption and popular culture acted to pacify the masses (Diggins 1994: 404). Their distaste for American mass culture was encapsulated in their portrayal of America as a 'totally administered society'. These views echoed Heidegger's attack on technology and rationality and pre-empted Foucault's power/knowledge distinction in Europe. These are examples of intellectuals' mission – the acquisition of knowledge – changing from emancipatory to imprisoning of the non-intellectual majority.

Ironically, unlike the social movements that emerged during this decade, there was a significant conservative current running through the output of some members of the Frankfurt School that Therborn (1998: 55–66) has described as a 'common and latent pessimism'. The purely intellectual current of critical theory emphasized the contradictions and negative aspects of modernity but offered no route out. Theodor Adorno and Max Horkheimer's *Dialectic of Enlightenment* ([1944] 1979) is a classic example of this in its unrelenting critique of the destructiveness of the Enlightenment. In this respect, these intellectuals shared none of the utopianism or optimism of the 1960s movements. The unity between the critical theorists and the 1960s activists was then paradoxical because it involved an alliance between an older generation of revolutionary defeat and a younger generation of revolutionary hope.

The contrast between the new social movements and some of the thinking of the Frankfurt School was highlighted most sharply by Adorno's controversial critique of jazz. At this time black music was an important part of the protest movements. However, Adorno turned this view on its head, arguing not only that jazz had no intrinsic aesthetic quality, but also that it was not an expression of social liberation for blacks. The tensions between the inactivity of the critical theorists and the activism of the students eventually surfaced in an ugly confrontation between the students and Adorno in Frankfurt. This episode in turn created divisions within the Frankfurt School itself, with Marcuse refusing to support Adorno's appeal to the police authorities. The students argued that the Frankfurt scholars, and Adorno in particular, were not following up the practical implications of critical theory and, implicitly, they charged that the academics' middle-class values prevailed over their radical opinions (Leslie 1999).

The nostalgic thread of critical theory seemed to be rooted in the theorists' experience of exile. After migrating to America, they steadfastly refused to integrate into American society. They maintained a distance from mainstream social science and refused to publish in English in favour of German. That this refusal had wider significance was evident in Adorno's contention that 'defiance of society included defiance of its language' (Jay 1973: 113–15, 176). This conservative tendency could have stemmed from their class location and, in particular, their middle-class Jewish background. Critics suggested that their middle-class and elite backgrounds had made them 'conservative' and anti-democratic. Being more of a populist, Edward Shils criticized Adorno's contempt for demo-cratic tastes and values. Critics saw his elitist views as reflecting his aspiration to 'European liberal-bourgeois society and the lifestyle of the cultured upper-middle-class members' (Jay 1986: 121).

However, the nostalgia and pessimism could more plausibly be traced back more specifically to the dislocations experienced by middle European Jews in the inter-war period. The deep-rooted pessimism in critical theory was embedded in these intellectuals' experiences as Jews and the rise of the Nazis that drove them into exile. This was decisive in the development of their views on American culture, forcing them to evaluate American mass culture as on a par with Nazi mass propaganda. The force of this experi-ence ran through all of their work as they examined the crisis of capitalism, the collapse of traditional liberalism and the rise of authori-tarianism (Jay 1973: 40). They became preoccupied with the question of how the Enlightenment and the civilizing process could have given way to fascism. It informed their preoccupation with anti-Semitism and racism that became the focus in studies such as Franz Neumann's *Behemoth* (1942) and the classic study *The Authoritarian Personality* (Adorno *et al.* 1950). The importance of the experience of Nazism on the intellectual output of the Frankfurt School was acknowledged by Alice Maier who recalled that

> We were all possessed, so to speak, of the idea we must beat Hitler and fascism, and this brought us all together. We all felt we had a mission . . . This mission really gave us a feeling of loyalty and being together.
>
> (Quoted in Jay 1973: 143)

Their experience of exile in America was significant to their outlooks, creating in them a feeling of being outsiders. The sense of being exiles in a foreign country was a persistent theme. They were concerned, for example, that their research on prejudice would whip up resentment at 'a bunch of foreign-born intellectuals sticking their noses into the private affairs of American workers' (Jay 1973: 225). Their exile status thus produced a strong conservative current, in the Mannheimian sense of nostalgia. Their generational experience of migration led to a culture shock – to negative perceptions of their experiences. Their critique of popular culture stemmed from their perception of it as a continuation of the propaganda machine they encountered in Nazi Germany. The Frankfurt School rejected German fascism, but could not fully accept American popular culture; as a result they tended to see American democracy as a sham.

In this respect their vision was essentially nostalgic. Thus the generational experience of Nazi Germany infused the Frankfurt School's way of looking at American society and their critique of mass culture. Adorno was central to this critique. He had been profoundly affected by the trauma of exile and this shaped his understanding of the post-war American environment, unleashing an uncompromising critique of mass culture (Jay 1986: 121). Memories of this experience plagued his thinking and influenced his perception of the protest movements of the 1960s. Opposing Marcuse's empathy with the students, Adorno said 'We withstood in our time, you no less than me, a much more dreadful situation – that of the murder of the Jews, without proceeding to praxis' (quoted in Leslie 1999: 127). Having suffered taunts and abuse from the students, Adorno's fear of the 'mob' or 'crowd mentality' that characterized the Nuremberg Rally was possibly heightened when the mob was led by articulate intellectuals (students) and contained elements from other classes.

The New York Intellectuals

Although the New York Intellectuals were not directly exiled like the Frankfurt School, they too constituted an intellectual generation forged largely by the experience of migration, immigration and depression. This group, including literary critics such as Irving Howe, journalists such as Norman Podhoretz and social scientists such as Daniel Bell, has been described as the 'most prominent formation of intellectual talent in mid-twentieth-century America' (Kennedy 1995: 8). The force of their impact on subsequent generations is apparent in the way studies by people such as Bell remain central to contemporary public and intellectual debate (Jacoby 1987: 8–9).

Initially the New York Intellectuals were left-leaning, criticizing American capitalism and arguing that the labour movement was critical to bringing about progressive social change. Bell originally adhered to the Marxist orthodoxy of America as a monopoly capitalist state. They had belonged to various socialist organizations: Bell had been a member of the Young People's Socialist League (Eyerman 1994: 169–71). Norman Podhoretz had been a socialist activist involved in the Trotskyist wing of the Young People's Socialist League and became one of its national leaders after it broke from the Socialist Party to become the youth group of the Socialist Workers' Party (Wald 1987: 312–13). Howe was a literary critic and editor of *Dissent*. Commentators have defined their earlier ideology as a combination of Marxism and modernism (Kennedy 1995: 8).

However, they became renowned for their shift from socialism to neo-conservatism and their abandonment of Marxism. Whereas in the 1950s and 1960s the Frankfurt School embarked on a wide-ranging attack on American society, arguing that its democratic institutions were a sham, the New York Intellectuals started to idealize its mixed economy and political institutions. By the mid-1950s Bell was starting to talk about the 'exhaustion of liberal and left-wing political ideology' for the analysis of contemporary America. He became famous for inventing the concept of a 'post-industrial order' and the idea that America was neither a 'capitalist' nor a 'mass' society but rather a society in which collections of groups competed for class, status and power, without any unifying ideal. His assessment of American society did not turn on the idea that it was riven by class conflict but on his critique of the unconstrained centralization of power (Eyerman 1994: 165–71).

This identification with America was rooted in the Cold War and developments in communism. The New York Intellectuals refused to denounce McCarthyism or America's role in Vietnam and they also opposed affirmative action for blacks and women (Waters 1996: 19). This transition from socialism to neo-conservatism was especially extreme in Podhoretz's case. When he became editor of *Commentary* from the 1960s he transformed the journal into a platform for opposing integration, affirmative action and homosexual rights and corporate dissociation from South Africa (Wald 1987: 354–5).

The shift was more ambiguous in the case of Bell, who describes himself as radical in economic theory, liberal in politics and a conservative in culture. Bell was most conservative in his approach to cultural issues, sharing with the Frankfurt School a distaste for popular American culture. He opposed the democratization of culture and relativist arguments about different cultures and has been accused of ignoring the worth of post-colonial politics or culture and attaching more value to 'elite–bourgeois–white–male–Western culture' (Waters 1996: 20). However, the movement away from a Marxist position to a Weberian one on American society was not in itself conservative.

The Cold War, which contrasted an apparent domestic stability with instability and repression in the Soviet Union, created a suspicion of ideology among various intellectuals. According to Diggins (1994: 401–2), during the 1950s and early 1960s a range of American intellectuals began to condemn communism with Reinhold Niebuhr presenting it as a 'mania of absolutism'; Arthur Schlesinger, Jr describing it as the curse of the 'monist and dogmatist'; Hannah Arendt talking about the 'tyranny of logicality'; Sydney Hook talking about the substitution of mystical 'faith' for 'critical intelligence' and Hans Morgenthau presenting the translation of 'universal principles' into 'utter depravity in action'. Bell fell into this category of intellectuals which, confronted by domestic stability combined with totalitarianism in the Soviet Union, started to challenge the feasibility of utopian ideas generally and Marxism in particular. He argued that America must remain free of ideology and adhere to its tradition of practicality.

The withdrawal from socialism was, therefore, the product of Stalinism. The Cold War forced intellectuals on the left to take sides and this generation chose the anti-Soviet side. It was during the late 1950s and 1960s that many of the New York Intellectuals began to challenge the notion of American imperialism (Wald 1987: 217). In *Land of Our Fathers* (1976) Irving Howe himself suggested that Jewish intellectuals turned rightwards after becoming disillusioned by communism and under the impact of McCarthyism (Jacoby 1987). Bell drew parallels between Stalinism and Nazism and he condemned left-wing intellectuals for refusing to see the similarities and for their overly romantic perception of Stalinism. He argued that they ignored the 'disparity between illusion and actuality' and the 'grubby reality of the sectarian party' (Bell [1967] 1996: 138).

However, the shift towards conservatism was also rooted in the impact of the post-war economic and social boom in America. The affluence that characterized this period had the effect of deradicalizing and professionalizing intellectuals – a trend that was critical to the political trajectories of this group and their rejection of radicalism. The New York Intellectuals were clear beneficiaries of these academic developments and their social mobility led them to view American democracy positively. Despite his earlier radicalism, Bell was later taken up in the wave of post-war professionalization and he became entrenched in mainstream academia. Irving Howe himself suggested that the changed status of intellectuals had undermined their oppositional status and instead led to their 'return to the bosom of the nation' (Eyerman 1994: 165–72). It was then the contrast between their privileged post-war status and their previous economically deprived backgrounds that led these thinkers to identify with the dominant American culture (Jacoby 1987: 90).

The generational experiences of migration and persecution were fundamentally significant in the shaping of this intellectual movement. Daniel Bell was born Daniel Bolotsky in 1919 in New York City from a Jewish family that had originally emigrated from Poland and Russia. Brought up in an immigrant Jewish ghetto during the Depression, he became politically active at an early age (Eyerman 1994: 171). Howe was born Irving Horenstein in 1920, the son of immigrants who ran a small grocery store that went out of business during the Depression, and Norman Podhoretz was born in 1930 in Brooklyn. This insecure background generated in them a desire to enter the more secure domains offered by their careers and their resistance to the democratization of culture followed from this. Reflecting on the New York Intellectuals' background, Bell said:

> The very nature of their [the New York Intellectuals'] limited backgrounds indicates that what really animated and drove them was a hunger for culture. In a sense going to college could be called a conversion to culture, coming out of slum or ghetto background and finding a whole world open that they had never known before.
>
> (Bell 1980: 131)

This sense of alienation and desire to 'get to the top' was also rooted in the discriminatory practices directed against Jews in immediate pre-war America that was evident in prestigious American universities. For example, in his memoirs, J. K. Galbraith (1981) recalls how Jews were systematically excluded from the highest echelons of the academic pecking order.

Thus, the combination of ethnicity and class had clear implications for this group's intellectual and political trajectory. Alexander Bloom (1986) carried out a historical study of the first and second generation of New York Intellectuals in terms of their accommodation to American society. Although born in America, the New York Intellectuals initially found an ambiguous place in American society. They were, or felt, rejected by American culture as Jewish and socialist. Daniel Bell, for example, recalls his sense of being an outsider and 'homeless' as a result of being both American and Jewish:

> I have found no 'final' place, for I have no final answers. I was born in *galut* and I accept – now gladly, though once in pain – the double burden and the double pleasure of my self-consciousness, the outward life of an American and the inward secret of the Jew. I walk with this

sign as a frontlet between my eyes and it is as visible to some secret others as their sign is to me.

(Quoted in Waters 1996: 17)

Irving Howe similarly recalled that he, Bell and others lived by a 'profoundly Jewish impulse' which was to 'beat the goyim at their own game . . . dazzle them a little' (Waters 1996: 17). The influence of ethnicity and class that deeply affected the New York Jewish intellectuals dovetailed with a definite sense of generational uniqueness and specificity (Podhoretz 1967).

It was the experience of the Vietnam war that propelled this generation of intellectuals into conflict with a younger generation that questioned the plausibility of the 'end of ideology' thesis when America's role in the war demonstrated that the country was far from ideologically neutral. Confronted by being drafted into the war, young Americans started to see tensions between America's ostensible commitment to democracy and its commitment to a venture that seemed doomed at a practical level. Thus the New Left started to see American policy as extreme and fanatical rather than rooted in traditional American pragmatism (Diggins 1994: 402).

These events precipitated a rift between the older generation of New York Intellectuals and newcomers. They showed disdain for new intellectual developments and popular music and expressed a nostalgia for traditional cultural values and practices. Hence they placed themselves between the culture of both the fifties beats and the sixties populism, both of which they saw as prosaic (Jacoby 1987: 69). Writing in 1968, Irving Howe claimed that they were being overtaken by a younger generation of intellectuals who had been 'unmarred by the traumas of the totalitarian age, bored with memories of defeat, and attracted to the idea of power' and thus lacked intellectual seriousness (Kennedy 1995: 16). These tensions were highlighted in their relations with Susan Sontag. Although she was associated with this group of intellectuals, her relationship with them reflected deep generational tensions. Sontag challenged the New York Intellectuals' attachment to high culture and they opposed her efforts to become intellectually independent, reflecting the way their generation had represented something of a 'boys' club' (Kennedy 1995: 7, 15). Thus, having defeated anti-Semitism, they were less interested in subsequent forms of discrimination and did not attempt leadership of other forms of social movements. This vacuum opened up the way for a separate feminist intellectual movement.

The Frankfurt School and the New York Intellectuals thus seemed, as a result of their experiences of migration and their Jewish identities, to adopt nostalgic and backward-looking thinking, especially in political and cultural areas. The nostalgia expressed by these intellectuals can be understood in terms of the theme of homeless generations. This pessimism can be contrasted with the more utopian and forward-looking outlooks of other members of this generation of intellectuals that were unaffected by migration. The Frankfurt School's pessimism and the New York Intellectuals' conservatism contrasted sharply with, for example, the stand of radicals such as C. Wright Mills or home-grown liberals such as Talcott Parsons (Holton and Turner 1986). In direct contrast to Bell, Podhortz and Howe, Mills argued that intellectuals should maintain a utopian vision and reject the conformism and apathy that had developed alongside their professionalization (Jacoby 1987: 117).

This optimism and forward-looking attitude could well have been rooted in the security of his American background. Although he came from similar economic backgrounds to the Jewish intellectuals, he did not share with them the experiences of migration that produced in them a sense of alienation. It is possible that it was his sense of security that enabled him, unlike the others, to sustain his radical predisposition (Jacoby 1987: 90–5). It is plausible to suppose then that the ethnic and exile consciousness produced by the generational experiences of Jews cut across the generational consciousness that might have united the Jewish intellectuals with contemporaries such as Mills. Mills, being more of an 'insider', raises the problem of one generation's successes making life too easy for the next which then becomes apathetic through the experiences of peace, full employment, careers and technological advances.

Edward Said: the Palestinian intellectual diaspora

Edward Said represents another diasporic generational response to America as a cohort of Palestinians thrust out of their own society in 1948 who prospered in America – the principal support of Israel. The traumatic event that shaped the course of Said's thinking was the formation of the state of Israel in 1948 and the consequent creation of homeless, stateless Palestinians. After the war, Palestinians either became refugees outside the new state's borders or fled to neighbouring countries, creating a Palestinian diaspora. Born in Jerusalem in 1935, Said was about 13 when the Jewish state was created.

Said's period as a doctoral student at Harvard paved the way for a brilliant intellectual career. After Princeton, Harvard and Stanford he became Parr University Professor of English and Comparative Literature at Columbia University. The impact of Said's thinking was so great that it could be understood as bringing about a paradigm shift in studies of the 'third world', influencing a whole new generation of historians and anthropologists (O'Hanlon and Washbrook 1992: 141) as well as literary criticism and art history. *Orientalism* (1978) probably had the most profound impact on intellectual thought. In it, Said looked at how western scholars talked about the orient and its populations, arguing that the way the orient was constructed had less to do with reality than with providing an epistemological justification for western authority over that region. He produced a school of thought that claimed that perceptions of Islam in the west were rooted in the material, political and cultural domination that accompanied western colonial expansion and, later, neo-colonialism. Said has also been accredited with transforming the perceptions of Arabs and Palestinians in the west, cutting through a climate that had previously equated Palestinians with terrorism and backwardness (Gilsenan 2000: 153).

The left disliked *Orientalism* because it departed from the political economy perspective and Said's use of concepts such as 'discourse' and 'power' (Gilsenan 2000: 152) had clearly been inspired by Michel Foucault's work. However, Said broke ranks with Foucault in his complete rejection of the latter's position of the role of the intellectual in political engagement. In contrast to Foucault, Said emphasized the emancipatory effects of knowledge as a basis for active political commitment and intervention. He argued that the role of the intellectual was not only to highlight systems of domination but also to dismantle them.

Through his work Said aimed to bring about real political changes and in this sense there was an utopian/activist strand to Said's thinking manifest in his political activism that started later in his career and was rooted in his personal experiences as an exiled Palestinian. As a representative of the Palestinian diaspora after the 1948 watershed, Said worked tirelessly for the Palestinian cause. His political activism was also rooted in the period of general political turmoil in the United States in the 1960s and it was from this period that he became most closely involved in the Palestinian cause. In 1969 and 1970 he visited Amman and Beirut, re-establishing contacts with relatives such as Kamal Nasser, poet and spokesperson for the PLO until 1973. In 1977 Said was elected to the Palestine National Council as an independent intellectual and, following the outbreak of the Palestinian Intifada in 1987, Said contributed to the translation into English of the Arabic text of the Palestinian Declaration of Independence in 1988. In 1992 he visited Palestine for the first time in forty-five years.

There was a dilemma for Said resulting from having prospered well in a country that overtly backed Israel in the succession of conflicts that have so catastrophically riven the Middle East. His way of dealing with this dilemma was to become a vigorous critic of American foreign policy generally and towards Israel in particular. Said's energies that resulted from being a Palestinian in exile underpinned a whole series of books on the Palestinian question. *Orientalism* was followed by his book *The Question of Palestine* ([1979] 1992) and *Covering Islam* (1981) which looked at contemporary western, especially American, coverage of the Middle East. Despite his work in other areas, such as literary criticism, it was as an intellectual Palestinian that Said became most well known.

The utopian aspect of Said's work was, however, tempered by a certain nostalgia. Despite being an American citizen as a result of inheriting it from his father, and a highly successful citizen, Said's personal experience of the Palestinian diaspora meant that he never fully felt American. He was a citizen in a country that throughout the post-war period was the main supporter of Israel, providing the country with strategic and economic resources. Running through his work there is a significant current of nostalgia and longing for the rebirth of Palestine combined with a deep regret about the historical events that led to the creation of Israel. Homelessness and nostalgia are persistent themes in his thinking, not simply in a factual sense, but also in a moral sense. What he seems to be saying is that the true intellectual emerges from a sense of not belonging and that it is only through the vantage point of homelessness and exile that an understanding of humanity can develop. In his autobiography *Out of Place: A Memoir* (1999) Said explores the tensions between his cultural and national roots and his educational experiences through the incongruity of the names 'Edward' and 'Said', where the first is the creation of his parents and the second the expression of his journey of discovery through displacement (Turner 2000a).

The experience of exile and not belonging was clearly very powerful in Said's case. Despite his successful integration into the intellectual life of America, he never quite seemed to feel accepted by the mainstream, particularly because he lived in the country that was politically deeply engaged with Israel. In the introduction to his *The Question of Palestine* ([1979] 1992) Said reflected on his feelings about writing the book:

> To explain one's sense of oneself as a Palestinian in this way is to feel embattled. To the West, which is where I live, to be a Palestinian is in political terms to be an outlaw of sorts, or at any rate very much an outsider. But that is a reality, and I mention it only as a way of indicating the peculiar loneliness of my undertaking in this book.
>
> (Said [1979] 1992: xxxxvi)

It was his experience of exile that 'permitted the beginning of a very protracted, unfinished process of self-realisation . . . New York was alienating, but it was an alienation that he could confront and refashion in ways that family life in Cairo had for years made impossible' (Gilsenan 2000: 157). The diasporic experience of Said as representative of the exiled generation of Palestinians was to produce a cosmopolitan outlook that celebrated homelessness. Homelessness and nostalgia are enduring themes running through Said's work, but this is not simply in a factual sense. Rather, Said seems to be proposing an ethical framework that suggests that being 'out of place' is critical to serious intellectual engagement and, moreover, that the experience of loss or exclusion, far from being negative, is what drives intellectual activity towards 'truth' (Turner 2000a: 126). This position tunes in with the thinking of the New York Intellectuals who, despite having a profound sense of alienation from American society and a deep-seated anxiety about 'fitting in' and 'outdoing' the insiders, seemed also to feel that it was their very status as outsiders that had been the source of their creativity.

Intellectual generations in post-war France

Intergenerational conflicts have been particularly important in shaping the structure of French intellectual thought, especially in the period following the Second World War. The French intellectual field was clearly a product of the peculiar circumstances of occupation and resistance (Judt 1992; Stoekl 1992). It is plausible then to suggest that the experience of war and occupation produced a negative current among France's post-war intellectuals – expressed in the existential philosophies of Heidegger and the early Sartre. Albert Camus ([1948] 1998, 1983) reacted to the destruction wrought by Nazi 'technological rationality' by focusing his novels on areas where knowledge and technological advance leave unchanged or exacerbate individual powerlessness – for example, emotional illiteracy which gets someone branded as a murderer (*The Outsider*) or a plague which isolates a town and benefits only its villains (*The Plague*).

The dislocations of the Second World War were critical to the intellectual development of France's leading post-war intellectuals, Jean-Paul Sartre (1905–80) and Simone de Beauvoir (1908–86), who made a dramatic contribution to the intellectual life of post-war France. They were of the generation that lived through both world wars. However, it was the Second World War, taking place when they were in their thirties, that had a particularly profound effect on them. The occupation of France and the

Vichy regime's collaboration with the Nazis were critically important to the shape of their subsequent political outlooks and activities. Dobson (1993) has described the Second World War as the 'turning point' in Sartre's intellectual life. Scriven (1999: 9–10) has commented that an understanding of Sartre's ideology depends on recognition that the Second World War was decisive: the wartime experience of defeat, occupation and liberation led to a complete overhaul of Sartre's thinking, forcing him to re-examine the principles he had constructed in the pre-war period. Sartre himself said:

> The war really divided my life in two. It began when I was thirty-four and ended when I was forty and that really was the passage from youth to maturity. At the same time, the war revealed to me certain aspects of myself and the world . . . You might say that in it I passed from the individualism, the pure individual, of before the war to the social and socialism. That was the real turning point of my life.
>
> (Sartre 1999: viii–ix)

In 1941, after being released from a prisoner of war camp, Sartre set up the monthly journal *Les Temps Modernes* with the explicit goal of developing a new post-war ideology (Davies 1987: 1). The effect of the war compelled him first to prioritize the role of the agent in historical change: the 'quest for the primary historical agent' was intrinsic to Sartre's post-war politics and philosophy (Scriven 1999: 8). He departed from structuralist accounts of history by arguing that disregard of the subject made an understanding of history impossible because 'it is the praxis of subjects that both creates the process and raises the possibility of its intelligibility' (Dobson 1993: 2). Sartre broke with structuralist Marxism, inventing instead a humanist version of the doctrine. By introducing agency into Marxism Sartre suggested that 'humanity was the author of its own history' and that through its actions it could take control of the historical process (Dobson 1993: 186).

The Nazi genocide of the Jews was especially important to Sartre's preoccupation with human agency and responsibility. In *The Anti-Semite and Jew* (1948) he argued that an understanding of the genocide of the Jews involved locating responsibility squarely with the perpetrators and complicit French people. Thus, he rejected the empiricist notion of anti-Semitism somehow resulting from the behaviour of the Jews (the 'blaming the victim' syndrome). The traumatic experience of genocide shaped Sartre's thinking on all subsequent conflicts. He strongly supported the creation of a Jewish state and remained committed to Israel in the post-war period. The 1967 Arab–Israeli war tested Sartre's sympathies because of his participation in the campaign for Algerian liberation. However, although torn by the conflicting demands of the two sides, he concluded that the French left had experienced the war as a 'personal tragedy' because people old enough to have experienced the German occupation knew that the systematic extermination of French Jews had resulted from the French people's 'passive complicity' as much as Nazi policy (Edmunds 2000: 143).

The sense of uncertainty generated by the war plausibly lay behind Sartre's preoccupation with 'universal historical truth'. His objection to relativism and focus on some kind of universal historical method provided him with the means by which to understand the past and inform the future. His dialectical method was totalizing in the sense that it 'applied to the process of human history as a whole' and that he believed that history was unified and that historical materialism as a method was 'the only truth of history' based on a rejection of relativism (Dobson 1993: 182). This framework seemed to be a way of ensuring some certainty after an experience of considerable flux.

Sartre's nostalgia was not, unlike the case of the Frankfurt School, fatalistic. There was also an optimistic thread running through thinkers such as Sartre that emerged in response to other traumatic events that directly touched France, in particular the protests against the Algerian war and the student movements. Like Said, Sartre was committed to the principle of intellectual political engagement. In *Les Temps Modernes* he assumed an 'anti-Flaubert' stance in his view that writers should be fully engaged in the political history of their time. After May 1968 in particular the journal became a major platform for intellectual critiques of contemporary French society (Davies 1987: 1–2). As Hazareesingh (1994: 54–5, emphasis added) has commented,

> Sartre typified the characteristics of the committed intellectual (*intellectuel engagé*). His conception of the intellectual's role emphasised the values of political radicalism and universalism. *Demarcating himself from the standard occupational view of the intellectual* he argued that intellectual activity was defined exclusively in the context of a particular project: the overthrow of bourgeois society. Thus the ultimate function of the intellectual was to reveal the class tensions inherent in capitalist society and prepare the ground for its destruction.

Sartre was thus at the vanguard of his generation, with his demand for political engagement by intellectuals serving as 'a model for emulation in intellectual circles until the mid-1970s' (Hazareesingh 1994: 55). This generation of intellectuals was distinguished by its commitment to challenging the existing social and political order. Throughout the 1960s Sartre campaigned in support of a variety of third world anti-colonial struggles. In relation to Cuba, Algeria, Vietnam and elsewhere he consistently backed indigenous populations' demands for independence from western domination (Scriven 1999: 14). He sympathized with the students' protests. In the early 1960s dissident intellectuals were involved in the protests against government policy in Algeria and supported the students' protests in the late 1960s. In the 1970s the French left threw its weight behind social movements such as feminism, regionalism and environmentalism (Hazareesingh 1994: 55–6).

Sartre was not, of course, of the same chronological generation as the students involved in the '68 events. However, he was at the heart of that generation in the lead he gave them with respect to political activism. Regis Debray described him as a 'transnational political intellectual who enabled his own generation to negotiate its way more effectively towards participation in practical politics'. Moreover, in recognition of the importance of generational experience, Debray drew parallels between his generation and Sartre's, suggesting that there was an analogy between the guilt experienced by Sartre in 1944–5 on discovering the atrocities of the Nazi concentration camps and Debray's own sense of shame in 1960–62 arising from an awareness of the systematic use of torture in Algeria. Confronted by these experiences Debray, like Sartre, became aware of the intellectual's inability to prevent such atrocities from occurring and became politically engaged as a way of absolving himself from the guilt. Debray claimed that Sartre acted as 'ferryman between the moralising attitudes of bourgeois rebellion and a more systematic participation in political projects at the centre of which was Sartre himself'. In this sense, Sartre provided a bridge between the pre-war and the post-war periods, acting as a political mediator for younger generations of French intellectuals (Scriven 1999: 11). In a sense, Sartre's whole intellectual career after the war reflected a desire to come to terms with France's past.

Like Sartre, the trauma of the Second World War profoundly affected de Beauvoir's intellectual development. Her experience of the war, and of French complicity with the Nazis, also had a direct impact on her thinking. One of the reasons why she was so disillusioned with the Soviet Union was the anti-Semitism of the Soviet government. Moreover, whereas before the war she had not been politically engaged, after the war she became more politically involved, supporting Algerian independence and campaigning against torture in Algeria and being generally involved in some of the political campaigns of the 1960s (see Evans 1985: 102–7).

However, de Beauvoir's generational consciousness was also an expression of her gender and a reaction against the oppression of her mother's generation. She is not remembered for her 'third world politics' but as a founder of western feminism through the publication of *The Second Sex* (de Beauvoir [1953] 1997). Having witnessed the exclusion of an earlier generation of women from the public realm, de Beauvoir set about creating a new intellectual current that demanded women's inclusion in the public realm, campaigning for economic and personal independence for women (Rodgers 1998: 60–1). *The Second Sex* was revolutionary in the sense that it promoted a radical change in the practices and values current in France at the time (Evans 1985: 99). It 'shocked a pronatalist, moralist France, and virulent reviews of the book dominated the press' (Rodgers 1998: 60–1).

De Beauvoir's status as a generational leader is demonstrated by the impact she made on 1960s feminism. Her analysis of women's status fed into the feminist movement as her ideas were 'transmitted, disseminated, propagated'. Thus, by the 1970s, ideas that had been regarded as beyond the pale in previous times, including the right to contraception, abortion, equal pay, and legislation against sexual harassment and rape, became generally accepted. Her status as a generational leader was also expressed in the way she became known as the 'mother of feminism' and successors described themselves as 'daughters of de Beauvoir'. She was described as the 'spiritual mother' of a generation of feminists who were both personally and intellectually inspired by her work. *The Second Sex* came to stand for 'the movement before the movement' and 'galvanised women's movements everywhere'; de Beauvoir herself said that 'At least I helped the women of my time and generation to become aware of themselves and their situation' (Rodgers 1998: 61–6).

The sense of rootlessness generated by the war (and combined in de Beauvoir's case with the powerlessness of being a woman) had a profound effect on this generation, leading to a desire to search for roots, for a concrete reality and for some kind of truth towards which actions should be directed. Thus, the ideas of this intellectual generation can be understood as a response to the trauma of the Second World War. Both Sartre and de Beauvoir then were members of an active generation because they had both the circumstances and an active ideology to bring about change. However, they could not remain hegemonic in the new historical context of the 1970s when uncertainties were replaced with stability and the (later) institutionalization of a socialist government under the presidency of François Mitterrand. This new historical and political climate provided the impetus to a new set of ideas. Within Bourdieu's (1988) understanding, change in the intellectual field occurs as a result of struggles between 'generations'. Intellectuals seeking to enhance their status will make strategic use of the circumstances presented to them.

It was this new political situation that led to a revision of the precepts of Sartre's generation. Until the early 1970s Sartre had been regarded as the 'unrivalled superstar of French thought' (Merquior 1991: 12). However, the mid-1970s marked a challenge to this dominant intellectual current and saw the emergence of rival intellectual currents such as post-structuralism and postmodernism and the rise of people such as Michel Foucault and Jacques Derrida who questioned the premises of contemporary intellectual, social and moral thought (Hazareesingh 1994: 62). Baudrillard (1983) was another figure who, in this context, challenged the possibility of traditional social theory and instead presented the world as simulated, in the sense that it involves representations of representations (Turner 1998: 5).

This paradigm shift in the French intellectual field can be illustrated through the figure of Michel Foucault (1926–84) who was at the vanguard of this new generation of intellectuals. Younger than Sartre, in the late 1960s Foucault taught philosophy at the university of Vincennes and in 1970 obtained the Chair of History of Systems of Thought at the Collège de France. He basically 'turned upside down' the ideas that were central to Sartre's philosophy (Merquior 1991: 14). His objective was to transform himself into 'another Sartre'. To this end, he rejected grand narratives and adopted a relativist position. His distaste for 'totalizing' historical methods was rooted in his rejection of the notions of causality and contradiction in historical evolution. Above all, he wanted to move away from formulating a 'global systematic theory which holds everything in place' in favour of a theory that focused on the 'specific mechanisms of power . . . to build little by little a strategic knowledge' (Walzer 1986: 51).

Also, in contrast to the previous generation of French intellectuals, Foucault claimed that intellectuals had no special role in politics. Foucault argued that ethical issues and scientific work were independent and that the intellectual did not represent the 'bearer of universal values' (Smart 1998: 401). He made a series of controversial anti-Sartrean statements and set out to shock the intellectual world by making extreme claims such as the 'death of man' at the end of *Les Mots et Les Choses* (Foucault 1966) as well as suggesting that Marxism belonged in the nineteenth-century episteme 'as fish in water' and was now entirely outmoded (Merquior 1991: 57).

This new intellectual language also fed into French feminism, leading the younger generation of feminists to challenge the universalist assumptions of de Beauvoir's feminism. Under the impact of thinkers such as

Foucault and Derrida feminists started to characterize *The Second Sex* as dated. They portrayed de Beauvoir's feminism as an 'intolerant, assimilating, sterilising universalism . . .' (Rodgers 1998: 67, 87–8). Such was the conflict between these generations that one member of the new generation saw de Beauvoir's death as an opportunity for freeing her own generation and 'speeding up women's entry into the twenty-first century' (Rodgers 1998: 67). Thus, the new generation of feminists overturned some of de Beauvoir's basic principles including her view that women's subordination was rooted in the differences between men and women and that equality would only be achieved once the social and cultural differences between the sexes were eradicated. In contrast the second wave of feminists promoted 'differentialism'. That is, they argued that only recognition of women's difference from men (such as their childbearing ability) could be the basis for any constructive change (Rodgers 1998: 87–8).

The difference between Sartre's generation and his successors seems to be rooted in the fact that whereas Sartre's engagement with war was direct (Second World War) Foucault's and Derrida's was vicarious (Vietnam, Algeria and so on). Sartre was driven to Marxism after realizing that his early existentialism was too solipsistic and offered no route to social integration. Existentialists were uprooted and searched for ways to reconnect with a stable reality (via a new view of consciousness and a Marxist framework for social integration). There was nothing for the Foucault/Derrida generation to do except refine the ideas of their predecessors or deconstruct/undermine them. They were frustrated that the real intellectual action came from outsiders and was anyway being eclipsed by non-intellectual direct action (over multinational companies, the environment and so forth). Moreover, Foucault had no direct involvement in the 1960s student movements and his journalistic writing on the Iranian revolution was as an outsider.

Thus Foucault did not want social integration. Rather, he and others of his generation enjoyed difference and nonconformity. Postmodernists celebrated technological rationalism, which ultimately expressed itself in Baudrillard's celebration of supermarkets and American 'culture'. Their reaction was to promote disengagement and a sense of irony from it rather than to get engaged and to see it as personally or socially challenging/transforming. This tendency for escapism culminated in Baudrillard arguing that the Gulf War never took place. For Baudrillard, signs, symbols and deceptive media meant the war was just a sensory illusion. The decline of universalism was inevitable as attempts at differentiation supplanted the previous generation's attempt at integration. After the loss of grand theory to fragmented and niche approaches there emerged a tendency for radicalism and conservatism to become blurred.

At the core of postmodern theory is a rejection of grand narratives. Moreover, the certainty associated with earlier social theory has been eclipsed by the social theorist's distance from the notion of truth and a tendency instead to doubt the authority of any final vocabulary about reality, including their own vocabulary (Rorty 1989). There is here a parallel with intellectual writers in the US: Hemingway, for example, said that the ultimate aim of a novelist was to write 'one true sentence'. Other war-affected writers such as Norman Mailer were similarly orientated. However, the next generation seemed to favour ambiguity and non-real events and descriptions – hence the rise of magic realism. Postmodernism as a social theory thus fed into fiction, undermining gritty realism and promoting escapism.

Thus, with the rise of postmodernism, the historic relationship between generations and ideas appears to be broken. There are no (new) intellectual generations of the 1990s and early 2000s. This is because the global Internet devolves discussion and undermines cohesive intellectual paradigms. While creating it (for research and publishing) intellectuals have also lost their leading roles as opinion makers through it. It has devolved downwards to non-intellectuals, professionals or the general public. Everyone can take part by posting ideas on the Internet so intellectuals' special use of this form of communication has been undermined. There are no big ideas, rather a proliferation of ideas, so it is no longer possible to rally behind any particular ones. The Internet links people according to interest rather than location, so it is therefore more cosmopolitan and in this sense there is some continuity with 1960s global intellectuals.

Conclusion

These case studies seem to suggest that various traumatic experiences and dislocations lead to a sense of rootlessness and nostalgia for stability. The intellectual generations thus affected by such instabilities set out to search for some kind of truth. However, once stability has been established, the later generations seem to find in this an unsettling restlessness that compels them to look for chaos. The trend thus seems to be that the post-war generation wanted social integration because they had seen earlier disintegration whereas the next generation wanted social disintegration because they have seen the monotony and oppressiveness of social integration underpinned by settled ideas in the political realm. In this sense there is an alternation between generations that put into place stable practices and institutions and the generations that follow this, which are left with no option but to challenge the established practices.

The big post-war discovery – that knowledge advance can be more constraining than liberating for society – created a crisis for the new intellectual generations who took up their posts expecting to transform society in a progressive way. The students in the late 1960s confronted them (in the case of the Frankfurt School) with the possibility that they could have helped to reinforce authorities that they had hoped to challenge and transcend. In this sense a 'free-floating' generation gave way to a subset of dominant class generation and the subsequent generation struggled again to become free-floating. These cases also seem to suggest that it is easier for outsiders to do this. So the most successful free-floating intellectuals in the 1950s and 1960s were Jews and exiles. In the late 1990s and early 2000s the most successful intellectuals are women, Asians, gays or people who have positioned themselves outside the intellectual establishment such as journalists, documentary makers and novelists. This trend seems to have resurrected the public intellectual of the type whose passing was lamented by Jacoby (1987). The differences in approach by these different generations suggests, moreover, that it might well be possible to synthesize the two distinct approaches to intellectuals offered by Gramsci and Bourdieu on the one hand and Mannheim on the other in the sense that the approaches can themselves be used to apply to different, alternate generations.

In conclusion, we suggest that war shaped intellectual consciousness in the twentieth century, especially the First and Second World Wars. Warfare, occupation and migration have then been fundamental to the construction of active and creative generations, and intellectual groups that fell between the wars were passive. Thus, twentieth-century thought has not been shaped by class, but by generational experience. Because generations rather than class shaped knowledge, Mannheim's view is more sociologically relevant than the legacy of Marx and Gramsci. Thus the history of ideas that has emphasized class or institutions (academics or universities) rather than generations is inadequate. However, experiences of rootlessness generated by migration (forced or voluntary) often created nostalgic intellectuals that moved from radicalism to conservatism as a result of the insecurity of their situation. Thus, creative intellectual generations of the twentieth century were paradoxically conservative.

Throughout this discussion of intellectual generations, women have been largely absent, apart from Simone de Beauvoir. This absence reflects the fact that prior to the 1960s there were only isolated cases of women intellectuals. In Britain, for example, elite institutions such as Cambridge and Oxford did not fully open up to women until the post-war period. Similarly in the US it was during the 1960s that there was a growth in women entering higher education, though there was still separation between the sexes on campus. In contrast, France had the culture of the salon and of women occupying more public space. This might explain the vanguard nature of de Beauvoir, though she was also unusual in having an intellectual upbringing. We would suggest that, as intellectual generations, women became more important in the post-1960s era, radicalized by anti-war protests, feminism, and post-war developments that gave them a more public role. It was during this period that women such as Susan Sontag in America, Martha Nussbaum, Germaine Greer and Juliet Mitchell in Britain came together in such a way that they could be described as an intellectual generation. For this reason, we shall be treating women separately in Chapter 5.

CHAPTER 4

Generations, national consciousness and intellectuals

An important aspect of our study is the role of generations in the formation of national consciousness. Studies of nationalism, nation states and national identity have rarely focused directly on generations. Yet, historically, generations as agents of revolutionary change have overwhelmingly been concerned with nationalism. Braungart (1984: 132–3), for example, has shown how all of the major movements concerned with self-determination, from the French Revolution to contemporary movements for ethnic self-determination, closely parallel four historical generations – Young Europe, Post-Victorian, Great Depression and the 1960s generation. The fact that all of these movements were based on a commitment to self-determination seems to support the view that nationalism and generational conflict often 'operate in tandem'.

Moreover, there appears to be a close relationship between revolutionary nationalist movements and younger generations and youth movements. Thus, in the Middle East, India and Indonesia, youth movements were, historically, critical to national rejuvenation (Eisenstadt 1956: 174) and Zionist youth movements in early twentieth-century Europe were also important to the construction of the new state of Israel. Developing first in

Germany and in central Europe, a variety of ideologically disparate youth movements were instrumental in forging a secular Jewish nationalism which, despite ideological differences, unified around the idea that Jewish emigration to Palestine was a prerequisite for national liberation. Between the two world wars they spread throughout Europe and in Palestine promoting an ideal of the 'new Jew' whose youthfulness and dynamism contrasted with the supposed traits of previous generations of Jews (Mayer 2000c: 289). A further important example would be the 'young Turks' in the construction of modern Turkey. The generic use of the term generation in this case suggests that this tendency is widespread and general.

We have therefore added a further dimension to Mannheim's (1997a) approach to generations, that is an exploration of the role of generations in nationalist visions. While the main distinction is between passive and active generations, it is also possible to imagine a special subcategory of active and strategic generations, namely patriarchal generations. A strategic generation that becomes harnessed to the creation of nations or at least to national or revolutionary movements is a generation of 'founding fathers'. This concept is particularly relevant because the phrase has generational connotations in the kinship sense. The traumatic events that appear to be particularly important for the formation of a politically conscious and active generation can be especially significant in forging a *national* political consciousness.

The strategic importance of particular generations that take maximum advantage of the social and material opportunities of their historical context is therefore often connected with nation building. These strategic generations can become particularly important in terms of political leadership. From a sociological point of view, political leadership is often closely bound up with the establishment of intellectual or cultural leadership. This idea stems from Antonio Gramsci's notion of hegemony, which suggested that the political leadership of a social class could never be achieved without moral leadership. In Italy, where the Roman Catholic Church shaped the world-view of the peasantry and urban working class, a socialist victory would require some degree of moral and cultural ascendancy. It is similarly possible to think about the role of generations and generational leaders in terms of intellectual leadership of their period. The issue of the political consciousness of generations appears to be very important in constructing the national consciousness of an epoch.

Because founding fathers promote mirror images of themselves, national consciousness tends generally to be masculine and to reflect the dominant national group. The idea that nations are formed in the shape of their founding fathers can also illuminate how they become exclusionary, especially towards latecomers, that is migrants. There is a wide range of illustrations of this tendency. Kemal Attaturk in relation to the formation of modern Turkey; President Tito in relation to Yugoslavia; and President Sukarno in the foundation of Indonesia. A further classic example of this trend is Israel. The overwhelming bulk of early Jewish immigrants to Palestine was from eastern Europe and it is in the image of the Ashkenazi Jew that Israel was formed. This is interesting because a division was established between the founders of the new state (Ashkenazi Jews) and Sephardi Jews (of Afro-Asian origin) whose emigration to Israel mainly started in the 1950s.

In terms of the creation and transformation of national consciousness, there are two routes to national integration. The first, 'constructed', refers to the construction of newer nations that are created out of cultural diversity and need, in the first place, to be based on a civic identity revolving around attitudes, beliefs and behaviours that anyone can share (US/Britain). However, because this invented and imposed unity has weak foundations, it is swiftly followed by attempts to unite the disparate groups through a sense of primordial belonging. The second type of nation formation, 'primordial', rests on shared culture, history and language (England/France). As migration starts to take a hold, the need to widen out and deconstruct the supposed primordial character of the nation becomes pressing. Generations of migrants who do not share the supposed shared traits of nations therefore play an important part in undermining the primordial claims and producing a more open version of national identity.

In this chapter we explore three main themes. First, we examine the role of generations in constructing and articulating national consciousness, especially through founding fathers. Second, we consider the argument that once new generations of latecomers are established, they may challenge the hegemonic and exclusivist national consciousness and seek to make it more inclusive. In the Mannheimian sense these new generations of minorities are important in overturning the status quo through their political activism. Their leaders are important in relation to strategic generations, because they provide a set of mentors who frequently stand in an adversarial relation to the dominant culture. These themes are illustrated through more detailed discussions of America and Britain. Finally, we explore the consequences of globalization on national identity and suggest that the 1960s generation, the first to be strategically involved in this historical trend, is integral to the emergence of cosmopolitan nationalism in the context of mass migration and the end of the Cold War.

America

The classic example of a founding generation is the group of men who were responsible for the leadership of the American revolution and the creation of the democratic constitution. In *A History of the American People* (1997) Paul Johnson noted that the formation of the American nation in the rebellion against British colonial rule had available an extraordinary depth of legal, military and political talent in such figures as John Adams (1735–1826), George Washington (1732–99), Patrick Henry (1736–99) and Tom Paine (1737–1809). There was also among them a slightly younger group: Thomas Jefferson (1743–1826), Alexander Hamilton (1755–1804), James Madison (1751–1836) and John Marshall (1755–1835). Through an experience of revolutionary struggle, this cluster of men forged much of the generative mythology that constituted American society and values as a point of reference for all subsequent generations. In Mannheim's terms, these people could be understood as the 'intelligentsia' whose purpose is to ensure that their interpretation of the social world becomes widely accepted. In relation to nationalism, this generation of political leaders was instrumental in constructing a particular nationalist vision that became deeply rooted in the popular imagination (Takaki 1990).

In the absence of a state religion, the Constitution became a sacred text of the American way of life, and the making of the American nation produced a national hagiography that has been constitutive of American civilization based on an 'imagined fraternity of white men' (Nelson 1998). There has been a significant drive to forge a homogeneous identity based on the Anglo-Saxon American through the marginalization of other cultures, a need that was especially pressing because the new American Republic was created out of a wide diversity of cultures as well as a North/South divide that could have collapsed into regionalism (Corse 1997: 27). This explained the moral purpose of the colonization of America and the subjugation of its aboriginal inhabitants. People such as Adams and Jefferson subscribed to the notion of Indian inferiority and barbarism and the superiority of the Anglo-American. Their speeches presented the indigenous people as nothing more than animals. While Jefferson favoured the legal termination of slavery, he believed that Africans were innately inferior to whites and had therefore to be colonized (Saxton 1990: 25–31). This strategic or founding generation set a political benchmark from which American history is measured in terms of tragedies or broken covenants (Bellah 1975) that are in some sense a departure from its foundation event and the founding fathers that made it possible.

Within American national consciousness, then, there has been a deeply rooted myth of white male supremacy that has fed into discriminatory practices against non-whites. From at least the eighteenth century the dominant national identity in the US was built on a politics of exclusion. The construction of American nationalism depended on defining slaves and Indians as culturally, morally and mentally inferior to white males. Replacing the old English monarchy with the new Protestant Republic involved exploiting a contrast between whites and non-whites where the former had a monopoly over virtue and the rest were presented as inferior. In the nineteenth century the supremacy of the Anglo-Saxon American through the nation building process was intensified through the subjugation of the American West, concretely and symbolically represented in the political celebrations surrounding the railroad push into the west along with the industrial revolution (Light and Chaloupka 2000: 333–5). This myth has been perpetuated in the importance of 'western' movies with cowboys as the 'goodies' and the Indians as the 'baddies'.[1]

As this was a newer nation, Americanness did not unite people until a shared culture was invented after long phases of historical fragmentation. Intellectuals' 'horizontalizing' mission therefore came right at the outset: they had to establish common values and unearth a supposed shared history to justify how those who share the same space can actually become a nation. The US is a paradigmatic case of this – a collection of proximate states assembled into a nation first by the Constitution then by the north's victory in the Civil War. Later generations of newer-nation intellectuals take on a second, 'primordialist' task – creating the national consciousness which ancient nations started out with, but which the newer nations lacked because they were founded on functional, intellectual principles. Hence, in the US, the constant effort by cultural commentators to identify 'American values' and by artists to write the Great American Novel. This became a priority once the US had run into its 'frontier' – no more states to add to the union so the task switched from 'widening' to 'deepening' its structure. The building of the nation required not just political independence but also a cultural unification. This need meant that the desire for the establishment of an 'authentic' American literature was articulated very soon after American independence. Thus, Nathaniel Hawthorne's *The Scarlet Letter* ([1850] 1983) and Herman Melville's *Moby Dick* ([1851] 1994) have come to be regarded as central to the original American literary canon (Corse 1997: 27–31). The special characteristics of the founding generation were firmly embedded in this cultural process in the formation of the state.

As we have already argued, warfare is often critical to the formation and transformation of national consciousness. In America the First World War acted to strengthen the founding version of American national consciousness. The political leaders central to this enterprise were presidents Woodrow Wilson (1856–1924) and Theodore Roosevelt (1858–1919). Confronted by major disruptions including migration and the repercussions of the Civil War, these presidents were integral to the growth of a national chauvinism that expressed itself in opposition to cultural diversity and hyphenated identities (Glazer 1997: 85). Both Wilson and Roosevelt saw the American national character, constructed between 1776 and 1787, as fixed and feared that immigration could dilute it (King 2000: 17–18). By ranking minorities according to their potential for assimilation, they actively contributed to the complete exclusion of African Americans and marginalization of other ethnic groups. It was the war that marked the onset of a new Americanization movement designed to marginalize cultural groups that did not fit into the ideal national type, allowing for little ambiguity or scope for blurring the national boundaries (King 2000: 90–1). At least until the 1950s, to be truly American was to be white and Protestant.

However, as we have suggested, strategic generations of 'newcomers' are important to transforming the national consciousness established by founding fathers. Generational conflict involves new generations challenging the norms and values of previous generations and these generations may be divided by gender or ethnicity. The experience of war was critical to the formation of generational consciousness among African Americans. Eyerman (2002) has identified three generations of African Americans, all of which were formed in response to the trauma of conflict and war. The first emerged in the aftermath of the Civil War and, through the use of a civil rights narrative, developed a model of freedom based on individual freedom and citizenship. The second developed in the aftermath of the First World War and aimed to reformulate African American identity around cultural and political nationalism. Although this generation was inspired by possibilities for integration into mainstream white society, it set out to create a particular cultural identity through a creative interest in black history, literature and art (Eyerman and Jamison 2000: 83–4). The third generation, formed after the Second World War and along with the decolonization of Africa, transformed the cultural patterns of the second into a more specifically political movement. The role of black soldiers in the military mobilized African Americans and this experience was a major influence on the civil rights movement in the later 1950s (Eyerman and Jamison 2000: 115).

It was this latter generation that was in a strategically well placed position to challenge and supplant dominant conceptions of what it meant to be American. This generation was able to exploit the international turmoil surrounding the Vietnam war and the drafting of black soldiers. It was the militarism of the period that paved the way for interracial mixing, which was one of the most significant legacies of the 1960s. The military demanded cooperation between 'races' and therefore helped to break down inter-ethnic barriers. This new kind of cooperation between Americans in Vietnam was portrayed in *Platoon* (Pratt 1990) in the scene where, with rhythm and blues music playing in the background, black and white, northern and southern male soldiers dance together. The Vietnam war therefore served as a catalyst for the integration of black culture into American society (Eyerman and Jamison 2000: 113–15).

However, the inter-ethnic cooperation demanded by the military was also tempered by the fact that black Americans were most badly affected by the war both at the front and at home (Marwick 1998: 543–4). Black soldiers were disproportionately represented in the US front line – often because many white Americans of the same age were better able to avoid active service. This succeeded in raising further black American consciousness and propelled into the public realm a set of intellectual black mentors who were instrumental in transforming the meaning of American identity. Among these, Martin Luther King was the most notable. He campaigned against the war and pressed for the civil rights movement to join with the peace movement to help end the conflict. Because the war was carried out in the name of American national identity this challenge represented the emergent consciousness of a generation of African Americans seeking to overturn the founding idea of American identity in favour of one that recognized cultural diversity. In the latter part of the 1960s a new generation of black activists emerged through the Black Power Movement and Malcolm X who adopted a different route. Impatient with the slowness of progress, black separatists opposed King's non-violent integrationist approach, portraying assimilation as a way of eradicating black cultural identity (Marwick 1998).

The peculiar nature of American society, and its segregation between blacks and whites, is precisely what provided the climate of success for such significant generational leaders as King and Malcolm X. Separation between whites and non-whites provided an obvious target against which new generations of minorities could express their opposition. Because, through the founding fathers and later generations of political leaders, American national identity was defined in such exclusive terms, the seeds were sown for a counter-movement among ethnic Americans, provoking the formation of a new politics that celebrated ethnic diversity. It was

Americans who had been marginalized by the 'narrow model of assimilation' that protested against it and campaigned for recognition. It was being 'written out' of American national identity that led this new generation of minorities to respond by promoting a new form of multiculturalism (King 2000: 257–9).

But what made this generation of minorities more strategically successful than previous ones was the fact that they could exploit an unprecedented series of traumatic events that mobilized large sections of the American public and gave rise to a wealth of social movements that identified with black politics. Thus it was 1960s America that was the watershed in terms of transforming the nature of American national consciousness. During this decade, the idea of America as a successful melting pot disintegrated, leading to a new politics based on ethnicity. This period marked the mobilization of a whole range of groups that challenged the dominant version of American national identity through, for example, the 'Race Pride Movement', which included Asian Americans, Indian Americans, Latinos and African Americans, all of whom wanted to celebrate their cultural traditions (King 2000: 257–67). Although hyphenated identities were probably invented in America in the mid- to late nineteenth century by free black Americans who described themselves as Afro-American (Eyerman 2002), it was not until the 1960s that they became more widely accepted.

The legacy of these generational movements has had a dramatic impact on American national consciousness. While discrimination continues to mark American society, the idea of hyphenated identities, such as African-American, seems to have become generally accepted and recognition of the diversity of a multitude of identities is now generally perceived as part of American national culture. Despite the continuing existence of voices calling for a retreat to a 'white or Anglo-Saxon' nation, such voices have been lost beneath the weight of support for multiculturalism as a way of understanding the American nation (Glazer 1997: 78–9). Thus, although conservative critics of the decline of the American nation have identified the 1960s generation as a social cause of cultural erosion, these generations of social protest can, in retrospect, be seen as crucial in the formation of contemporary Americanness.

The United Kingdom

One of the difficulties with any discussion of the formation of British national consciousness is that, unlike America, it had no easily identifiable founding fathers.[2] Moreover, its relationship with Englishness means that there is little consensus among historians over the origins or nature of British nationalism, making it an even more slippery concept.[3] Nevertheless, the formation of modern Britain may be associated with the wars against the threat of Napoleonic domination in which the heroic activities of Horatio Nelson created an enduring image of Britain as an island of liberty surrounded by a European threat. After the Boston Tea Party and the loss of the American colonial states, Britain emerged successfully from the encounter with Napoleonic France to become the dominant industrial and colonial power of the nineteenth century. Nelson's naval triumphs created the context of British military supremacy in subsequent colonial struggles. After the battle of Trafalgar, Nelson became a symbol of national survival. Imperialism and warfare was also integral to English nationalism. According to Kumar (2000a: 588–9), Englishness was an imperial nationalism in two senses: first, because it created the core of Great Britain and second, because it created an overseas empire in North America, the Caribbean and later in India and South-East Asia. Warfare and conflict have then been the defining features of both British and English nationalism, reflecting the close association between nationalism and masculinity, a theme that has been ably demonstrated by Mosse's (1985) work on European nationalism and sexuality.

People born in Britain in 1890, 1920 and 1945 were confronted in their youth with radically different issues and life chances simply by virtue of their date of birth, but the social processes by which they become the generation of the trenches, the Depression and the post-war boom are not factually given. Rather, these cohorts become generations through the social significance of the periods in which they lived. The generation of men who took part in the First World War contributed to a strong sense of national identity. The destructive consequences of the First World War for the generation that entered the trenches in 1914 have been extensively documented in social history. The savage impact of military technology brought into question the traditional institutions that had underpinned European societies in the modern period – family, church, monarchy and the universities. While the church and monarchy that had been the social glue of British constitutional history since John Locke and the 'glorious settlement' of the late seventeenth century have been damaged as plausible roots of social legitimacy by war and its consequences, the crown remains an important constitutional component of 'Britishness' (Nairn 1994).

The inter-war generation was denied this sense of national belonging and could therefore be described as the 'lost generation'. In Britain, the protest against the technological war of the trenches produced a nostalgic vision of a traditional England in which youth might be allowed to flourish without the control of a corrupted older generation. In retrospect, the poetry of the First World War was a sad product of a generation of public school boys and their shattered patriotism and masculine aspirations. The literature of this period involved the destruction of the tranquil, nostalgic and rural world of the Georgian poets. The poetry of Rupert Brooke (1887–1915) most perfectly captures this mood. Although Wilfred Owen's poetry expressed the despair of war, Brooke emerged posthumously as the vibrant symbol of youthfulness and England (Hassall 1964).

The oscillations between war and prosperity provide the context within which one can understand generational changes through the perspective of English literary expression. The twentieth century was a century of social and economic decline, and that English (literary) culture expresses those social transformations through the medium of literary reflection. While Britain's decline may be measured from the Great Exhibition of 1851, the erosion of military, economic and intellectual leadership since 1900 has been dramatic and fairly continuous. There are various ways in which one might characterize that decline of influence, but Ralf Dahrendorf's phrase 'decline without fall' is useful in expressing the gradual but ineluctable downward direction of British industry and British influence (Dahrendorf 1982). If the Conservative Party has been the main political vehicle of traditional patterns of English identity, then the absence of major involvement in war after 1945 may explain both the decline of Tory culture and the erosion of Englishness. Changes in the role of Britain in the global economic and political system are closely connected to changes in British nationalism and self-confidence. The recent process of devolution of powers in Britain is perhaps the final stage in the break-up of robust Britishness that has been connected with Nelson and the destruction of French naval power as a threat to the British Isles.

As a result of internal colonialism (Hechter 1975) English identity became the dominant core of Britishness. It was the English who became most closely identified with new Great Britain that became, essentially, Greater England (McCrone and Kiely 2000: 26), and who asserted dominance over the periphery. Whereas imperialist nationalism, such as British, tends not to stress ethnic origins but political or cultural or religious factors (Kumar 2000a: 579–60), Englishness has traditionally emphasized a supposed ethnic identity. It has therefore been particularly hostile to outsiders, including indigenous populations under colonialism, the Welsh, Scots and Irish, and women. English stereotyping of the Celts involved a view of them as backward, uncivilized and unable to govern themselves (Dodd 1995: 2–12).

Historically, then, English national culture has contained within it a significant conservative current. The conservatism of English culture was perhaps best expressed in the inter-war period by an American, T. S. Eliot (1888–1965). In *The Waste Land* (1971) Eliot captured the mood of conservative despair with western society that was denied any possibility of redemption. Eliot's commitment to high Anglicanism produced a conservative view of education and authority that he expressed in *Notes Towards a Definition of Culture* (1949) in which he defended a hierarchical grading of culture as a necessary condition of democracy. Eliot was criticized by Edmund Wilson who found Eliot's classicism, royalism and Anglo-Catholicism implausible as the basis for a social theory of English culture. Even in Eliot's commitment to Christianity Wilson saw a religious doctrine 'uninspired by hope' (Wilson 1952: 437). Like his contemporary Ezra Pound, Eliot's Englishness was in essence an attempt to escape from the vulgarities of urban America into the landscape and religious practice of the seventeenth century (Perl 1989).

English nationalism also involved the subordination of the cultures over which the empire expanded through imposing on them an ideal of Englishness. Literature in these schools involved teaching the English classics. Thus schoolchildren in the West Indies were compelled to read Wordsworth's 'Daffodils' in the Queen's English (Lauret 1999: 124). The pre-British empire English literary canon also held out an ideal of English identity whose perpetuation and sustenance depended upon England's colonial interests abroad. Jane Austen's *Mansfield Park* ([1814] 1996) is a good illustration of this in that the very maintenance of Mansfield Park depended upon the holding of plantations in the West Indies (Said 1994: 95–115).

As we have already argued, nationalist imagery and rhetoric tends to be hostile to 'latecomers' or migrants. British society was transformed in the 1950s as a result of large waves of immigration from the new commonwealth. In 1968 Enoch Powell made a speech about what he thought would be the disastrous consequences of further immigration into Britain. Powell was an English nationalist; an 'ethnic essentialist' in that he believed that human beings fell into primary groups sharing communal features that were deeply rooted linguistically and ethnically. He saw the English as one of these groups, that is, a homogeneous community sharing political traditions based on inherent English values of fair play and tolerance. He felt that these characteristics were specifically English and that English people were born with them; that they could not be acquired simply by living in England (Ignatieff 1998: 18). Powell also thought that free market economics could reinvigorate the economy and give a new sense of national pride. He was also a traditional academic who deeply regretted the trend within universities towards vocationalism and commercialism, even though this was the necessary consequence of his free market ideology.

It is possible to argue that British nationalism started with Nelson and ended with Powell's 'rivers of blood' speech. Made in the context of decolonization and the collapse of the British empire, the speech was a response to the realization that British nationalism was over. It can be understood as a last call for forging a strong national identity in the face of Britain's collapsing international status. Powell paid a heavy political price for making this speech and this partly reflected its timing. It was made precisely in the decade that had seen mass protests against colonialism and imperialism. It was a political timebomb less in a domestic sense, because it was generally recognized that his concerns touched a chord with many people (Heffer 1998: 457), than in an international sense because it went against the grain of the international climate of the time. As Ignatieff (1998: 18) has pointed out, the political class of 1968 was critical to turning the tide against Powellism and ostracizing Powellite discourse. It was the idea that England stood for a community of civic values rather than ethnic origin that won the debates set off by this speech, changing the very way people thought and talked about national identity and race.

The legacy of Powell's thinking continues to be found among contemporary commentators and intellectuals whose nostalgia for the past surfaces through the notion that a strong national identity depends on internal cultural unity and cohesion and an opposition to multiculturalism on the grounds that it damages the national character. Thus intellectuals such as Roger Scruton and Anthony Flew echo Powell's views in the pages of the *Salisbury Review*, a journal that has provided a forum for the traditionalist, nostalgic views of what it means to be English. Moreover, Powellism pre-empted Thatcherism, though in a way Thatcherism showed up the contradictions inherent in Powell's stand, namely the need for migrants to maintain the economy and the need for a reinvention of universities based on market principles. The election in September 2001 of Iain Duncan Smith as Conservative leader in the immediate aftermath of the terrorist attack on New York is interesting because his military background was assumed to be particularly relevant as Britain prepared for the possibility of war. But it has also emphasized the historical connection between Englishness and militarism.

As in America, it was a generation of 'latecomers' that played a critical part in transforming traditional views on national identity in response to the use of supremacist notions of Englishness in political discourses (Asad 1993: 239–68) and in undermining the notion that English identity was primordial. However, the whole pattern of minorities' challenge to British/English national identity, while sharing the same generational location, differed sharply from the American case. There were no equivalent figures to Martin Luther King or Malcolm X. Instead, it was a generation of intellectual minorities who transformed popular thinking about British and English national identity and they did this in a less combative way than in the US, with professional academics, politicians, lawyers and artists and writers pushing for change in a more gradual fashion. As Werbner (1991) suggests, prominent leaders such as Luther King tend to emerge from circumstances of considerable crisis, such as the anti-colonial struggles and civil rights movements.

The UK case contrasts with this. Many political initiatives were locally inspired, though gaining some national momentum such as the Rock Against Racism Movement and the Anti-Nazi League, that emerged in reaction to Powellism (Werbner 1991). Many creative initiatives among minorities were carried out in a local way, with artists using ethnic communities as a source of creativity (Bhattacharyya 1999: 78). There is also a strong tradition of writers and artists who articulate the needs of marginalized groups, such as Ben Okri, Hanif Kureishi and Zadie Smith. However, Salman Rushdie and other literary figures made a national impact. The controversies surrounding the publication of *The Satanic Verses* (Rushdie 1988) were above all about what it meant to be British (Ahmed 1992). What the Rushdie affair brought into sharp relief was the tension between the British civic tradition of tolerance and commitment to multiculturalism. The post-war liberal elite that had espoused cultural relativity was caught up between the need to recognize other cultures and to impose limits on that recognition. It resurrected the Protestant aspect of British national identity and brought on to the political agenda the question of the relationship between church and state in a so-called secular society (Ignatieff 1998).

Other post-war minorities who played a part in transforming British/English national identity included a series of high-profile politicians. In politics, there is Bill Morris, Paul Boateng, Dianne Abbott, the late Bernie Grant and Trevor Phillips, who recently became chair of the new London Assembly. After his death, Grant was replaced by David Lammy, a well-educated young black lawyer, as the MP for Tottenham. There has also been some high-profile lobbying among professional minorities, especially through, for example, members of the Society of Black Lawyers, who can translate raw protest into the official language – for example, Rudi

Narayan after the Brixton riot and Imran Khan who represented Stephen Lawrence's family.

Black intellectuals started to put questions about minorities and national identity on to the political agenda – including, most obviously, people such as Stuart Hall, Paul Gilroy and Kobena Mercer and Hazel Carby, all of whom were associated with Birmingham University (Lauret 1999: 130). Hall and Gilroy were two of the most prominent members of a new generation of minority intellectuals to challenge prevailing ideas about British/English nationalism. They were involved in the production of landmark books such as *There Ain't No Black in the Union Jack* (Gilroy 1987); *Policing the Crisis: Mugging, the State and Law and Order* (Hall *et al.* 1978) and *The Empire Strikes Back: Race and Racism in 70s Britain* (CCCS 1982). Gilroy wrote about the 'invisibility of "race"'' in cultural studies and opposed the kind of nationalism that seemed to involve a 'morbid celebration of England and Englishness from which blacks are systematically excluded' (Lauret 1999: 135, n8). Hall argued against the closed, exclusive and regressive form of English national identity that was integral to contemporary racism, claiming that Thatcherism provided fertile ground for the growth of an English identity that systematically excluded minorities (Hall 1992: 259, n1).

Hall and Gilroy were therefore critical to the break with the prevailing orthodoxy that identities were somehow fixed, natural and inevitable, arguing instead that national identities are historically constructed and malleable. They rejected any notion of national or ethnic identity being somehow primordial or 'in the blood'. The impact of their intellectual output was formidable, influencing a whole later generation of social scientists and providing the core to an academic base in 'race relations' with Warwick, Bristol and Birmingham becoming centres for studies in this area. Although they were not chronologically of the same age, they were of the same generation in that, in the two cases, their political views had been forged by the experience of Powellism and its aftermath.

It is ironic that while Hall and Gilroy have been identified as major critics of British culture, they have emerged as mainstream representatives of a specific generation of British intellectuals. Hall has reproduced the Englishness of his generational location (Rojek 2001). Gilroy explicitly identifies himself as English and suggests that, with time, there is scope for minorities in the UK to use the hyphenated appellation Black–English instead of Black–British. It could be argued that just by talking publicly about English identity Hall and Gilroy gave the mainstream view a voice because previously it was a national identity that seemed to have no name. By being the first to tackle Englishness directly, these minorities defined themselves into it through their rejection of a discourse that would otherwise exclude minorities.

They had also been influenced by events in America even if they could not adopt the same strategies for change as black American leaders. This new generation of intellectual minorities had been involved in the 1960s movements. Hall engaged in New Left politics and forged links with intellectuals such as Raymond Williams and Raphael Samuel who were involved in the *Universities and Left Review*. During this period he became involved in left activities such as CND and he has explicitly defined himself as being at the vanguard of the 'post-1968 new politics'. His interest in colonial issues and identity as a West Indian at Oxford University led him to present himself as 'part of the first generation, black, anti-colonial or postcolonial intelligentsia, who studied in England . . .' (see Chen 1996: 492–4).

An important question raised by these developments is the extent to which they become incorporated into the political mainstream and popular consciousness. There is some evidence that the ideas espoused by these people have gained a strong position in contemporary elite thinking, having found their way into traditional British institutions such as the BBC. This organization's vision for the twenty-first century turns very much on the celebration of diversity and multiculturalism and suggests that the BBC's role is to explore the meaning of Britishness in a multicultural devolving Britain and that the culture of the organization itself needs to embrace ethnic minorities.[4]

The key differences between the US and Britain and the different patterns of generational response rest, obviously, with the different histories of the two countries. The rise of populist generational mentors such as King and Malcolm X and later Jesse Jackson happened in the US because America had both slavery and the Civil War, and an almost apartheid style of relations between whites and non-whites which meant that the latter had a very obvious target to attack. The US had more open confrontations because of the extent of discrimination and also, ironically, because the founding fathers' declarations about justice and the constitution meant there was some kind of external yardstick against which minorities could judge their status. Much of the US had a form of apartheid until the mid-1950s; it was only systematically tackled in the Kennedy/Johnson era and it informally continues in parts of the south. That gave ethnic minorities something to protest about and created a whole generation that could be receptive to the appeals of Luther King or (much later) object to the treatment of Rodney King.

In Britain, this extreme form of institutionalized racism did not exist.

Discrimination was subtler and regionally differentiated and affected different minority groups with different degrees of severity. Arguably, Britain's more urban culture also gave racial minorities a relatively more cosmopolitan setting in which they could be shielded from the more prejudicial small-town attitudes. Another particular feature of post-war history in Britain is the absence of a powerful racial ideology and powerful fascist groups. Although British society is undoubtedly racist, fascist parties such as the British National Party (BNP) have failed to win any formal political support. Racial riots in northern England in the summer of 2001 were the exception rather than the rule and their causes were not exclusively racial.

This situation partly reflects the nature of the British electoral system and, later, the rise of Thatcherism, which satiated the far right's appetite for racism. However, it remains true that Powellism really failed and that Thatcherism is the closest there has been to a hegemonic racist discourse. The racist right in the UK has made none of the inroads into either the political or popular domain made by the far right in France, for example, partly because the Conservatives, under Thatcher's leadership, stole the far right's thunder. The Conservative Party was then unique as a nationalist party with racist elements that stayed mainstream and thereby squeezed out the far right parties.

Moreover, this generation of minorities lived through a period characterized by higher education/expansion and economic boom. While social mobility in Britain for ethnic minorities is not straightforward, with some minorities doing better than others, there has been the growth of a professional black middle class and there is a perception of wider opportunities for minorities in Britain, which has not had the caste relations seen in America. The UK has had visible waves of immigrants (e.g. *Empire Windrush*) leading to clear generational divides. The first generation settles for any kind of work and looks up to white English culture; the next generation, whether successfully integrated or not, sees flaws in England and wants to do more than the previous generation.

Thus, in both America and the UK there is evidence that generations of latecomers or migrants played a critical role in transforming the traditional national identities of their respective countries, deconstructing the notion that national identity is somehow primordial and introducing the notion of hyphenated national identities. This trend is deeply rooted in the US but has emerged also in the UK through the notion of, for example, Black–British, though this hyphenation has not yet been extended to English identity, revealing the continuation of the idea of Englishness as being more ethnic than Britishness (Ignatieff 1998). These original transformations started in the 1960s before the onset of globalization. In the following section we shall suggest, however, that this generation of minority intellectuals is now playing an important part in inventing another identity that both accepts and transcends national boundaries through the concept of diaspora. This will be illustrated largely through a discussion of British intellectuals.

Globalization and the cosmopolitan intellectual

The current climate of globalization and the end of the Cold War has created an historical impulse towards redefining national identity as national boundaries have become blurred. There is a current of thought suggesting that globalization has threatened communities and sown the seeds for fundamentalist or 'closed' nationalisms. The pessimistic view of globalization is that, although globalization has facilitated international access to the same goods and technology, these have become detached from social organization and, as a result, there has been a growth of groups asserting various identities, many of which are fundamentalist and inward-looking (Touraine 2000). One has only to think about recent events in the Balkans, Africa and a host of other places to see evidence of the worst kinds of nationalist conflicts. Globally, there are signs of new expressions of racism, mainly directed against Muslim minorities, with international organizations such as NATO portraying Islam as a threat in much the same way as it identified communism as a threat in the Cold War period. The attack on the World Trade Center in New York appears to have been a product of the fundamentalism and the polarization of the rich north and the impoverished south. The attack has become a powerful symbol of anti-globalization.

However, we want to suggest that as a result of multiculturalism, massive migration, countries with multiple cultural traditions and countries being drawn into global trade, intellectuals are becoming global carriers of cosmopolitan values and cosmopolitan virtue. The issues of national identity, internationalism and cosmopolitanism become especially acute in the case of migrant or diasporic intellectuals. Multiculturalism, the Hispanic presence and diasporic academics may in fact create the conditions for cosmopolitanism. The growth of new global communication systems means that intellectuals may find themselves in new roles as mediators between local and global cultures and carriers of cosmopolitan virtue, which is characterized by irony, emotional distance, scepticism, secularity and an ethic of stewardship (Turner 2000b). Intellectuals, and especially minority intellectuals, are playing a part in creating new cosmopolitan identities that are a version of benign nationalism (see Edmunds and Turner 2001). These identities are opposed to any form of exclusive nationalism but accommodating towards benign or soft nationalist sentiment.

In connection with Britain, the post-war generation of intellectual minorities are now, in the context of Britain's possible 'break-up' combined with European integration and globalization, starting further to transform our understanding of national identity. As well as Hall and Gilroy, there are other migrant intellectuals such as Couze Venn and Pnina Werbner who are helping to shift conceptions of national identity in the contemporary context of globalization, and reinventing the idea of diaspora as a positive rather than negative identity.

Whereas Hall originally resisted using the term diaspora because of its association with the idea of the Jewish diaspora and the Palestinian question, he more recently started to make links between the Jewish experience and the black diaspora. Noting the tendency for African American writers who metaphorically use the Jewish experience to express their own situation, he has drawn parallels between the narrative of Jewish historical experience and that of colonialism and slavery (Chen 1996: 491). Hall now argues that what used to be called 'alienation' can be positively transmuted and that

> post-coloniality, in a curious way, prepared one to live in a 'postmodern' or diasporic relationship to identity. Paradigmatically, it's a diasporic experience. Since migration has turned out to be *the* world-historical event of late modernity, the classic postmodern experience turns out to be the diasporic experience.

Hall's initial pleasure at being in England later gave way to a sense of alienation:

> I knew England from the inside. But I am not and never will be 'English'. I know both places intimately, but I am not wholly of either place. And that's exactly the diasporic experience, far away enough to experience the sense of exile and loss, close enough to understand the enigma of an always-postponed 'arrival'.
>
> (Quoted in Chen 1996: 487)

Elite members of this generation of minorities are, then, introducing a new sense of belonging that both accepts and transcends national boundaries through the concept of *diaspora*. Instead of seeing this identity as associated with passivity and victims, they are celebrating diasporic identities as a positive part of contemporary life. Gilroy has suggested, for example, that diasporic status is positive because it offers an alternative to the idea of natural self-conscious nations with tidily drawn boundaries. Instead, he suggests, diaspora problematizes the 'cultural and historical mechanics of belonging' and undermines the location of identity with particular territory. This overrides the negative history of diaspora that has involved people being forced to migrate as a result of violence (Gilroy 1997: 328). Both Hall and Gilroy are mobilizing their own diasporic status to challenge traditional notions of Britishness or Englishness and to ensure the inclusion of postcolonial cultures. Their sense of distance from traditional British identity has given them an idea of national identity as negotiable (Stratton and Ang 1996: 383–4).

This sense of diasporic identity stems from their biographical backgrounds of migration and rootlessness. As we have already noted, Hall was born in Jamaica and migrated to England in 1951. Both Hall and Gilroy spent a lot of time in the US and Gilroy is now a professor at Yale University. Pnina Werbner is an academic who was born in Johannesburg then migrated to Israel where she did her first degree, and later came to Britain. Couze Venn, also an academic, was born in Mauritius and came to Britain in 1962. These experiences have led them to import various concepts into the UK, including the notion of the 'diasporic intellectual', associated with Stuart Hall, and ideas such as that of hybridity, associated with Gilroy and Homi Bhaba (Lauret 1999: 130). The impact of their cosmopolitan experiences has also led to the introduction of hyphenated identities for minorities as a positive way of dealing with the flux of national identity and to generate a sense of inclusive belonging. Stuart Hall, for example, introduced the idea of 'new ethnicities' and cultural hybridity, offering a critique of 'ethnic absolutism' and advocating cultural openness. This insistence on openness also involved a rejection of 'black' absolutism (Modood 1994: 872–3).

These intellectuals tend to have a very weak sense of their own national identity, while simultaneously recognizing others' right to national self-determination. Nationalism is a project they pursue on behalf of others, not a passion they pursue for themselves. With respect to their own sense of national identity, they feel cosmopolitan, variously describing themselves as 'global citizens', 'mid-Atlantic' or 'postcolonial':

My sense of identity has changed over the years and was not always significant. For example, in the sixties and early seventies the mode was more that of internationalism, so national identity did not seem to matter . . . I think of myself as postcolonial, thus belonging in a fractured way to an ex-colonial space, and a space that is yet to emerge.

(C. Venn, interview 2000)

Moreover, they feel that their global or cosmopolitan identities are anti-nationalistic in an extreme sense. They feel comfortable with the diversity of their roots and celebrate a cosmopolitanism – their own variable backgrounds have given them a sensitivity to cultural diversity and a drive to promote tolerance for benign national identities. Pnina Werbner said:

> I have connections to three countries. Two countries very strongly, Israel and England, and also to Africa because I've spent time in Africa . . . At a kind of sentimental level, I have very deep roots in these three places . . . But as a stance on my own position now, I've become very cynical about all nationalism. *So I see myself as a sort of floating world citizen, I suppose. I don't really have – I'm not willing to defend a country.*
>
> (P. Werbner, interview 2000, emphasis added)

What these intellectual minorities have in common is an espousal of a universalist framework that embraces benign particularisms and objects to malign expressions of particularist identities. Gilroy's latest study, *Between Camps: Nations, Cultures and the Allure of Race* (2000), is a treatise precisely to end what he describes as 'ethnic absolutism' not just of whites but of blacks too. Instead he offers a vision of identity that transcends absolutist nationalist visions and celebrates both cosmopolitanism and universalism summed up in his concept of planetary humanism. It shows him putting forward a utopian vision in his suggestion that politics based on colour need to be transcended, largely through European cosmopolitanism, though his exhortation to move beyond nationalist identity politics does not involve lapsing into bland cultural uniformity. Gilroy objects to any form of extreme nationalism, including that of extremist, separatist movements such as the Nation of Islam, drawing parallels between such movements and fascism. He is promoting instead a loose multiculturalism:

> Uncoupled from its associations with unbridgeable, absolute difference and reconfigured with a wider sense of the unevenly developed power of subnational (local) and supranational relations, multiculturalism can force nationalism and biosocial explanations of race and ethnicity into more defensive postures.
>
> (Gilroy 2000: 244)

Thus, while members of this generation are subscribing to universalist principles rooted in their variable experiences, they are nonetheless endorsing benign forms of particularism. They are seeking to push European integration away from reactive pan-European racism (especially anti-Muslim) towards a more open identity. Their generational experiences have made them particularly conscious of the regressive aspects of Europe. Minority elites therefore have some reservations about Europe. Their reticence is rooted in both personal and collective memories of the atrocities committed in the past against minorities, notably the genocide of the Jews. They are promoting a New Europe that will come to terms with what happened and seek to ensure that nothing like that can ever happen again. They worry that the insecurities generated by change will bring to the fore latent xenophobia; that the new Europe could regress into the past and provide opportunities for the reawakening of xenophobia.

Gilroy, for example, is cautious about Europe and concerned about the creation of a 'fortress Europe' but at the same time he sees the potential for a vibrant multiculturalism and cosmopolitanism:

Today, in Europe at least, there is less justification for [this] stark . . . diagnosis. The erstwhile barbarians are within the gates and may not live in a formally separated ghetto or enclave. The frontiers of cultural difference can no longer be made congruent with national borders. The cities do not belong exclusively to the colonisers and their kin. Isolated areas in which elements of colonial social life persist and thrive and can be identified, *but these urban worlds draw their vitality and much of their appeal from varieties of cultural crossing–mixing–moving – that demand the proximity if not the presence of the other.*

(Gilroy 2000: 249, emphasis added)

In the new context of European devolution, globalism and devolution, this generation of minorities are now playing a part in constructing a national consciousness that is cosmopolitan in its multiculturalism and openness and tolerance for diversity.

Conclusion

Although there is a current of thinking that globalism/localism and cosmopolitanism/nationalism are two extremes, a position that is both cosmopolitan and sensitive to benign expressions of local identity and multiculturalism seems to be emerging. The 'break-up of Britain' offers scope for the transformation of identities. In this context, some key minority representatives of the elite who grew up in Britain in the post-war period are offering positive narratives and seeking to shape the public agenda on nationalism and national identity in the new historical/political context. These narratives are cosmopolitan in their adoption of identities that transcend national boundaries, such as 'global citizen'. However, such universalist concepts are being combined with tolerance for benign local and national identities.

The question is: what are the conditions that generate a benign nationalism, which is tolerant of local identities, multiculturalism and so on? There is evidence of a generational effect, reflecting the peculiarity of the fifty years that this generation of British minorities has lived through. First, there has been a relative absence of violent colonial wars in post-war Britain. Although there was the Suez war, it paled into insignificance next to, for example, France's war with Algeria. Macmillan's 'wind of change' speech was revolutionary in a sense because he said that Britain would be prepared to give Africa back rather than fight in a drawn-out guerrilla war. Britain therefore got rid of its colonial past quite peacefully. Despite the presence of ideological divisions between left and right, the post-war conservative governments' policies involved relinquishing colonial territories and granting independence without resistance.

In contrast the Americans were bogged down in Vietnam for years. Similarly, French politics were trapped in the colonial struggles over Algeria. However, in the latter part of the post-war period, Americanness could not be successfully sustained through the exclusion of internal minorities because they had become integral to the country's economic success. At this point, American national identity was forged more through the identification of external 'others', such as communism during the McCarthy era and Islamic fundamentalism (and the World Trade Centre attacks). American national consciousness in the latter part of the twentieth century defined itself in opposition to countries such as Russia, China, Cuba and Nicaragua.

What seems to be happening then is that migrant intellectuals, in the context of globalization and through the experience of migration, are again transforming the parameters of national identity. Their espousal of benign forms of national consciousness seems to be rooted both in their generational location and their ethnic backgrounds. As a generation, this cohort was fed a whole range of attitudes based around tolerance for difference. This generation was forged by the experience, either directly or indirectly, of migration into post-war Britain. Many of the people discussed here are part of the first generation of migrants to Britain. They were born (mostly) in the years surrounding the Second World War, reaching their twenties or thirties in the 1960s. They all shared a generational consciousness of this time: their recollections were centred around the events of the sixties – the Vietnam war, the women's movements, anti-colonialism and so on. They adopted the values of the era in their progressive outlook towards issues such as colonialism, 'race' and feminism.

The post-war generation of intellectuals have become more interconnected and interconnecting – through international networking, electronic communication and the operation of 'brain drains' in various directions. The unsettled lives of twentieth-century academics – often moving across borders to escape repression, seek intellectual inspiration or better pay – reinforces their drive to make links across national boundaries and to distrust nationalistic identities. This has led to a global intellectual whose very rootlessness alienates them from extreme forms of nationalistic feeling. They want to find a source of identity/integration that does not rely on gut nationalist feeling. Intellectuals tend to share a language (technical) with foreign colleagues, and have become progressively better networked with their foreign counterparts.

These debates provide possibilities for a new generation to reject Cold War intellectuals, pro-American apologists or nostalgic migrants. The mobility associated with globalization has particularly affected intellectuals. There is emerging a new generation of intellectuals for whom national identity is becoming less central. Several leading intellectual minorities in the UK, for example, have migrated to America or Australia. What characterizes the type of thinking promoted by the new 'cosmopolitan' intellectuals is their unwillingness to accept any national authority and, rather, to celebrate a new kind of diaspora. The post-war generation of migrant intellectuals is now playing a part in redefining ideas about national identity largely through the concept of diaspora. They are more optimistic in the suggestion that there may be no necessary connection between globalism and reactionary localism. The character of new forms of local or national identities in the context of globalization may be more open-ended.

In conclusion, social scientific explanations of nationalism have developed significantly in recent years. However, the specific contribution of generational change and experience has been neglected. From an historical point of view, generations have been crucial to the construction of national consciousness both in terms of the role of founding fathers and subsequent generations of newcomers who, once integrated, actively start to challenge national definitions that exclude them. The 1960s generation of migrants in countries such as the US and Britain have been particularly important in creating national identities that are cosmopolitan and tolerant.

However, the recent attack on New York has already created a new generation. Globally people will define identities in terms of this single catastrophic event. The racial debate that has followed the bombing, pitting the west against Islam, will severely test the trend towards global cosmopolitanism. Anti-globalization may begin to destroy the possibilities of benign nationalism as a new generation emerges that has been shaped by the image of falling towers of the World Trade Center. But we suggest that this generational consciousness of global terror will eventually be challenged by the generation that did not exist on 12 September 2001.

Notes

1 In his response to the terrorist attacks on the World Trade Center in September 2001 President George W. Bush invoked traditional American westerns in his call for Bin Laden to be captured 'dead or alive', thus expressing a nostalgia for the nationalist consciousness formed by the founding fathers.
2 Tom Paine, John Locke and John Stuart Mill probably come the closest but whereas the first took his political activism abroad the others were not politically engaged.
3 For a discussion of the relationship between Britishness and Englishness see Langlands 1999.
4 CRE Press Release, CRE Race in the Media Awards, 7 April 2000.

CHAPTER 5

Generations, women and national consciousness

In Chapter 4 we examined the role of generations in forging national consciousness and suggested that generations may be culturally generative in political life. We argued that founding fathers tended to construct a national consciousness that was a mirror image of themselves, that is, patriarchal and hostile to 'latecomers'. However, subsequent generations of migrants played a critical part in deconstructing the original founding myths of nationhood. Thus, groups from the margins may be important in transforming mainstream national consciousness. In this chapter, we suggest further that later generations of women also from the margins (in terms of their contribution to founding nationalist myths) play a similar role to latecomers in deconstructing dominant nationalist imagery.

Reiterating our model of generational change, we suggest that traumatic events such as wars create active generations that are defined by a shared generational consciousness. Active generations sharing such a consciousness often shape national consciousness and this is captured in the idea of founding fathers. Intellectuals play an important role in articulating and constructing national identity, which is why intellectuals are defined generationally. Traditionally, in the course of nation building, founding fathers have filled this role. Thus, gender is important because (masculine) generational consciousness tends to push women to margins in the sense that their role is defined for them by the founders. This means that at this stage they are passive generations, having to acquiesce to the dominant mode of thinking. However, subsequent generations of women (once they have the appropriate resources) become active generations when they seek to overturn traditional national narratives. Our theory is that traumatic events shape generational experiences in such a way as to generate nationalism. However, women's experience of these traumatic events differs from men's and active generations of women (empowered by political and social changes) generate a new form of national consciousness that is less aggressive and exclusive than that constructed by founding fathers.

Women and nationalism

The generational concept of founding fathers is relevant because it has strong patriarchal connotations as well as generational overtones. Nationalism and the formation of national consciousness have historically been infused with patriarchalism. There is a considerable range of historical and cross-national illustrations of the masculinist current in nationalist ideology. In Napoleonic France women were prohibited from wearing the tricoleur cocarde (rosette), a nationalist symbol during the French revolution, in order to keep this patriotic symbol respectable (Gilligan 1982). The founding fathers of the new state of Israel promoted a masculinist nationalism based on a male cult of heroism (Mayer 2000b: 15). American national identity constructed in the post-revolutionary period rested on the idea of 'white manhood' excluding both minorities and women (Nelson 1998). Contemporary debates about the inclusion of homosexuals in the armed forces in America testify to the controversial nature of transgressing the masculine norm of national militarism and how deeply entrenched it is in political culture (see Allen 2000).

In times of heightened nationalist conflict, the subjugation of women is especially pronounced, often involving direct control over women's bodies. There have been cases in Ireland, for example, when women have been prevented for terminating pregnancies after being raped (Martin 2000: 65–85). In very extreme warring situations the raping of women (though not officially condoned) is routine. Thus in the case of the former Yugoslavia men routinely raped women from the opposing side (Mostov 2000: 89–112). Reflecting on his wartime experiences, a Vietnam war veteran recalled that 'having sex with a woman and then killing her made one a double-veteran' (Greer 1999: 210).

The tendency within nationalism to denigrate femininity and hold up masculine values as ideal seems to be universal. However, we would suggest that the use of masculine symbols and imagery tends to be more pronounced in newer, constructed nations because of the insecurity surrounding their formation. Thus during its nation building phase Germany was particularly aggressive, being constructed out of a series of formerly independent states in 1871. Russia similarly signified its construction as a communist nation with the symbol of the hammer and sickle and through propaganda that focused on soldiers and farm workers. While older nations such as France also have strong masculine currents, they tend to use symbols that are female to signify the nation – in this case, Marianne and Joan of Arc. Britain and England do not neatly fit this typology, because Britannia has been the traditional symbol of the constructed nation Britain. However, there remains an interesting contrast between the masculine, British figure of John Bull and the feminine symbol of Englishness expressed in the idea of the 'English rose'.

Despite the extent of this empirical evidence of a connection between nationalism and patriarchy, the classic texts on nationalism have paid very little attention to this issue. Gellner's (1983) analysis of the relationship between modernization and nationalism did not consider women; Hobsbawm and Ranger's (1988) analysis of the invention of nationalist traditions failed to explore how these traditions were essentially male projects. And Anderson's (1983) work on nations as imagined communities did not explore how half of the population was not imagined in them or the different ways in which women were imagined. George Mosse's (1985) work on nationalism and homosexuality ended this trend with a pathbreaking analysis of the way nationalist narratives have denigrated femininity.

During the 1980s there was a proliferation of studies on women and nationalism by authors such as Enloe (1989), Yuval-Davis and Anthias (1989) and Nagel (1998), all of whom have focused on different aspects of the relationship between women and nationalism. Enloe, for example, was interested in exploring images of women under imperialism and the role of women in international relations. Yuval-Davis and Anthias (1989) were more concerned with exposing the ways in which women have been central to national projects by looking, for example, at how women act to reproduce national collectivities physically, symbolically and culturally. They also explored the role of women in third world nationalist projects. The aim then was to uncover the part women played in nationalist movements that was absent in conventional approaches to nationalism. While the concept of 'founding mother' seems odd (testifying to the deep-rooted patriarchal nature of founding nationalist movements) there are some examples of women playing high-profile roles in building national consciousness, perhaps the most notable being Indira Gandhi and Benazir Bhutto. Though it is interesting to note that these women were the grand-daughters and daughters of founding fathers.

Nagel (1998) has adopted a different perspective, suggesting that analyses of women and nationalism should concentrate less on uncovering their role in nationalist projects and more on what seems to be an integral link between nationalism and masculinity. She suggests that although women do play a part in the formation of nationalist consciousness, they remain 'supporting actors' and it is men who 'write the scripts'. Notwithstanding the proviso about founding fathers' daughters and granddaughters (Bhutto/Gandhi), the absence of women in nation building is why the concept of founding mothers has not gained popular currency.

There is then a consensus of opinion claiming that nationalism and patriarchy have been closely related. In the creation of national consciousness, women have been objects rather than subjects, passive rather than active. However, although it seems plausible that nationalism and masculinity are essentially related simply by virtue of the apparent universality of patriarchal nationalism, the connection is not a necessary one. Our argument is that there is an important connection between generations and nationalism and that new generations and generational shifts can bring about significant changes in the content of nationalist consciousness or narratives. In Chapter 4 we demonstrated this by exploring the role of migrant generations in transforming founding national consciousness. In this chapter we suggest that with changes in women's position and their greater involvement in the public sphere[1] women are starting to write the scripts and they could change the face of national consciousness. Through the greater availability of resources, post-war generations of 'marginal groups' (minorities/women) are transforming nationalist narratives and the 1960s generation, for historical reasons, has been especially active in this respect.

Feminist generations and oppositional nationalism

As we have argued, wars are critical to the creation of generational consciousness. However, generations are not unitary. The concept of generational unit, introduced by Mannheim, suggests that the various voices of a given generation may be stratified according to political orientation. It is also possible that generational consciousness forged by traumatic events could differ according to variables such as gender or ethnicity. As Schneider (1988) has suggested, women's experiences of traumatic, generational events may differ from men's. It therefore follows that the generational consciousness of women, created by wars such as the First World War, has specifically gendered aspects: women tend to pick up the pieces after nationalism drives men to excess, for example through nursing casualties, by working as military auxiliaries and by replacing the male workforce on farms or in munitions factories while men are at war.

Historically, women have been excluded from the elite and the national narratives thereby constructed by founding fathers have generally reflected their own masculinity and marginalized women. Because women have tended to be left out of the nation building process, it could be argued that as a group they have traditionally been nation-less and therefore more inclined towards internationalism and empathy with women of other nations even if they are part of the 'enemy'. Women leaders who have managed to reach a position of influence have often articulated inter-nationalist positions. For example, Rosa Luxemburg was unique as a woman to reach the top of a socialist movement. As one of the leaders of the German communist movement who was executed in 1919, Luxem-burg relentlessly promoted an internationalist perspective, prioritizing her universalist principles over other identities.

Moreover, there is a strong connection between feminist generations and opposition to extreme (especially militaristic) expressions of national-ism. The generational experience of traumatic events seems to have played a role in the creation of different feminist generations and a feminist reaction against militaristic nationalism. There are clear links between war, feminist generations and pacifism or oppositional nationalism. The First World War was critical to shaping feminist consciousness in the immediate post-war period. It gave feminism a 'harder edge' and intro-duced a 'thread of strong, well-articulated pacifist feminism' that fed inter-war pacifism among women (Kamester and Vellacot 1987: 1). Traumatized by the loss of lives in the First World War, the generation of first-wave feminists led anti-nationalist and pacifist campaigns promoting internationalist and universalist principles.

Women have been prominent opponents of unjust wars and excessive militarism, and feminist movements in particular have frequently allied themselves with pacifist movements. First-wave feminism in the US, for example, was linked with various peace movements and there was an integral relationship between feminism and the anti-slavery movement

(Humm 1992: 2). This generation of feminists was critical to the formation of later women's peace groups such as Women Strike for Peace
(WSP). The women involved in it had lived through the Great Depression,
the rise of fascism in Europe and Asia, the Second World War and the
Holocaust and Hiroshima (Swerdlow 1993: 2–5).

The generational experience of war was also an important factor in the
development of second-wave feminism and its anti-nationalistic and
universalist character. The rise of the Women's Liberation Movement in
the late 1960s had direct links with other liberation movements, especially
those of national self-determination in the colonies. The term 'women's
liberation' delineated the new movement from earlier feminist movements
by stressing a connection with the liberation movements of the 1960s to
which it was allied. Women's Liberation was closely connected to the
black power and student movements and the post-colonial liberation
movements that were transforming political life (Caine 1997: 255–60).

International conflict in the 1960s, especially the Vietnam war, thus
created a new generation of feminists that participated in anti-nationalistic and pacifist movements. While both generations shared the same outlook on nationalistic wars, it was not until the 1960s that women were in
a position to influence the political agenda. Thus in 1960s America
women's movements fused with anti-war campaigns. Prominent American
women played an important part in opposing American nationalism and
neocolonialism. One of the most notable examples was Susan Sontag
whose intellectual rootlessness led her to adopt an ironic sense of what it
meant to be American and an uneasiness with nationalism. Involved in
the feminist and anti-war campaigns of the 1960s, she became a strong
critic of American foreign policy and the idea of American national
supremacy, accusing America of suffering from a violent 'national psy-
chosis' and dissociating herself from American neocolonialism (Kennedy
1995: 62–5).

In Britain the experience of the First World War produced a generation
of feminists that adopted a pacifist, internationalist perspective. This conflict highlighted the link between feminist interests and peace, with many
feminists arguing that the subordination of women was linked with
militarism and adopting an internationalist perspective (Caine 1997: 217).
The anti-nationalist current among this generation was manifest, for
example, in various anti-fascist activities (Humm 1992: 5). Women were
also at the forefront of pacifist and internationalist activities in the British
Labour Party. During the 1920s and 1930s it was women who were the
'great peace crusaders' and active in the No More War movement. For
example, Labour women such as Jennie Lee and Ellen Wilkinson actively

joined with feminists such as Vera Brittain in the international Women's Committee Against War and Fascism (Graves 1994: 208–9).

Second-wave feminism in Britain also arose in an important sense in response to the generational impact of international conflict, in particular the Vietnam war and the role of American feminists in the anti-war movement. In Britain, second-wave feminism developed in response to the growth in women's liberation in America: the anti-war campaigns, the civil rights movement and so on. Well-known members of this new feminist wave, such as Sheila Rowbotham and Juliet Mitchell, have explicitly acknowledged this heritage. For example, Rowbotham recalls that her political engagement began with her involvement in the Vietnam Solidarity movement in 1966: 'I had heard about the women's movement in the United States and met American radicals through their opposition to the Vietnam war' (Rowbotham 1990: 34).

While first-wave feminism was actively linked with peace movements, the later movement was responsible for broadening out peace activism to include arguments against both the direct violence of war and indirect violence through, for example, the impact of militarism on the third world. The pacifism of the second wave also extended to include campaigns against domestic violence against women. So although first-wave feminists were deeply involved in peace campaigns, it was the second wave that was instrumental in creating broader ways of expressing anti-militaristic practices in campaigns such as the protest at Greenham Common (see Humm 1992: 296). Nineteen sixties feminism was committed to national self-determination for the colonies, anti-apartheid, anti-racism and the Campaign for Nuclear Disarmament (CND).

Women and patriarchal Britishness/Englishness

British and English nationalism have traditionally contained strong masculinist currents, mascots and narratives. At the point of its construction, British national identity was defined largely in opposition to femininity, expressed in its portrayal of its main 'other' (namely France) as effeminate. British national rhetoric protested against the assumed 'femininity' of French culture and celebrated British culture for its masculine traits, including rationality and pragmatism. Moreover, it was felt that the national character could only be maintained through the existence of separate spheres: whereas men belonged to the public sphere, women belonged to the private sphere (Colley 1996: 265–7). Thus men demonized the enemy (talking up stereotypes in the public sphere) while women empathized with the casualties of the enemy in private. The equation between Britishness and masculinity was given concrete shape in the symbolic figure of John Bull.

In contrast to British nationalism, English nationalism was traditionally a cultural rather than political phenomenon. The salience of Englishness over Britishness has varied historically. Before the collapse of the empire and the end of colonialism, British identity was possibly more salient than English identity; though at different historical moments attempts to distinguish Englishness became a priority. Like British nationalist consciousness, traditional English nationalism also contained an anti-feminine current. Although it defined itself largely in terms of its opposition to the 'peripheral' communities, that is the Welsh, Scots and Irish, Englishness also excluded women. Being largely articulated at the cultural level, this masculine side of Englishness was expressed mainly by evoking male cultural activities (especially public school ones) such as cricket (Walder 1990: 171).

In the post-Second World War period, especially during the 1970s and 1980s, a new form of Englishness developed. Although it drew on ideas of earlier concepts of English identity, it differed from these versions in that ideas about Englishness were increasingly used for political purposes. During this period New Right Conservative politicians, starting with Enoch Powell, started to espouse an English identity that was politically exclusionary towards the Welsh, the Scots, the working classes, minorities and women (Kumar 2000b: 17–18).

This shift from cultural to political expression reflected various changes in post-war Britain. Migration was one of the most important factors in this. However, changes in women's role in the economy and men's dominance in typical male areas such as public schools, universities, the church, the army, the media and trade unions were also important. Moreover, the shift towards post-industrialism, which led to a decline in characteristic male occupations and growth in the service industry, also ended with the idea of men becoming redundant. These developments might have created a sense of insecurity that expressed itself in the resurrection of masculine forms of national identity.

In Britain, women have been important in opposing masculine and militaristic nationalism and promoting internationalist and universalist principles. This internationalist perspective was most famously articulated by Virginia Woolf (1882–1941) who was actively involved in the pacifist Women's Cooperative and refused national honours. Radically objecting to the masculinist aspect of nationalism, Woolf argued that women should reject men's hold over the nation and see the 'whole world' as their country

(Walder 1990: 171). In *Three Guineas* ([1938] 1991) Woolf explored the relationship between male power and militarism, claiming that women should distance themselves from the authoritarian and militaristic values of patriarchal society (Humm 1992: 21) and believing patriotism to be part of men's rather than women's 'instinct'. Moreover, she argued that women should not be patriotic because they had been excluded from the structures of English society; they were in this sense 'outsiders' and she argued that England did not belong to women. In suggesting that women should distance themselves from patriotism, Woolf said a woman should remind herself '. . . of the position of her sex and her class in the past . . . of the amount of land, wealth and property in the possession of her own sex and class in the present – how much of "England" in fact belongs to her' (Woolf 1938).

In the 1960s and 1970s a new generation of women intellectuals developed the themes of internationalism, universalism and pacifism. This generation included Germaine Greer, Sheila Rowbotham and Juliet Mitchell. Greer was born in Australia but remained in Britain after doing a PhD at Cambridge. In 1970 she published her controversial book *The Female Eunuch* ([1970] 1981). Following the publication of 'Women: the longest revolution' in the *New Left Review* in 1966 Juliet Mitchell went on to publish *Woman's Estate* in 1971. At the same time Sheila Rowbotham explored the relationship between women and the left and pressed for mutual cooperation between socialists and feminists (see Rowbotham 1990).

Much of what this generation of feminists said about nationalism was implied rather than explicit. However, one of Greer's principal interests had been how to transcend national boundaries between first and third world women. She was also concerned with the need for peace and for feminism and pacifism to combine in opposition to cultures of violence (Greer 1999: 205). This generation of feminists, internationalized by the experience of war in third world countries and movements for self-determination in the colonies, were wary of nationalist expression in their own countries. Thus Rowbotham opposed the narrow English sentiment personified in the thinking of people such as Enoch Powell and recalls how Powell's speech and the rise of racism had led her to join the 'International Socialists'.

Because of its close links with the left, this generation of feminists was committed to universalist principles. Echoes of Virginia Woolf's position on women and nationalism emerged in the late 1960s in the pages of the magazine *Nova*. Here, in an article entitled 'How Do You Plead Mrs John Bull?', Irma Kurtz, for example, urged 'Don't be nationalistic females, join the big sorority . . . you are a woman . . . we are compelled to be women' (quoted in Connolly 1995: 152).

During the 1960s visual images through the mass media were globally circulated in an unprecedented way. It was during this time that children being killed by warfare started to be publicized internationally, affecting western conceptions of conflict. This theme was exploited by protesters against the Vietnam war through the slogan 'Hey, hey LBJ, how many kids did you kill today?' Then there was the famine in Biafra that provided the world with images of starving children. Children's deaths are the ones (in war) that generate most emotive publicity. Resistance to violent conflict by women reflected their role as carers, especially as mothers. It may be that women have tended to be particularly affected by children being part of the collateral damage of warfare. This theme continues to be articulated today by women who took part in the 1960s protests. Greer (1999: 208) has expressed this concern, suggesting that

> . . . war nowadays is waged by virtually invulnerable professionals against extremely vulnerable civilian populations. In modern warfare women and children on the ground are in greater danger than the professionals who maim and kill from a distance without risk to themselves.

More recently, Greer became active in a group formed in 1999 to oppose intervention in Kosovo. She addressed public meetings and used the media to protest against the west's role. Echoing themes used in protests against the Vietnam war, Greer suggested that contemporary intervention reflected an old imperialist desire by the west to intervene in other countries' affairs. Women's involvement in the 1960s movements may also explain the emergent shape of peace movements. For example, the 1960s CND leadership was male and UK-focused. However, in the 1980s under Joan Ruddock's leadership the organization became more internationalist and started linking up with other groups, broadening the debate and engaging in forms of protest other than marches.

1960s women today and cosmopolitan Englishness

Recent developments in the UK have provided an opportunity to explore the connections between women, generations and national identity. In contemporary Britain, there is now a space opening up for the creation of a new English identity. Devolution, European integration and globalization have compelled a rethink of regional identities generally and Englishness in particular. Because of the role of the elite in opinion shaping, it is possible to argue that 'new cultural intermediaries' are critical to structuring post-war cultural attitudes (see Featherstone *et al.* 1991). As we have suggested, generation intellectuals, including academics, opinion leaders, cultural commentators and journalists, play an important part in innovating in the ideological and cultural realm. We have suggested further that they play an important role in constructing national narratives.

As we have already shown, it is generally acknowledged that the post-war generation ('baby boomers'; 'sixties generation') has been critical to social, cultural and political changes in the second half of the twentieth century. However, very little attention has been paid to this generation's effect on national consciousness despite the fact that the 1960s movements were principally concerned with national self-determination. Moreover, there has been an equivalent neglect of the role of 1960s women in transforming national consciousness. An important question is whether, having reached maturity and entered the public realm in an unprecedented way, women of the sixties generation are having any impact on current thinking on national identity. Have the values, forged in the generational experience of the 1960s, affected contemporary thinking on nationalism and national identity?

In an earlier research project (Edmunds and Turner 2001) we found evidence that women from the post-war British elite are contributing to the construction of a new English national identity that is more open, tolerant and cosmopolitan. They are espousing a forward-looking *creative* national identity – they are actively promoting a break with traditional Englishness in their rejection of supremacist attitudes and in their celebration of cultural diversity, Europeanness and expressions of Welsh and Scottish cultural and/or national aspirations.

Whereas traditional Englishness was defined in opposition to and as superior to Welsh, Scottish or Irish nationalism, this new way of thinking about what it means to be English involves embracing the principle of national self-determination for the Celtic nations and rejecting notions of English supremacy. It suggests that the English have for too long subjugated these nations and that aspirations for autonomy or independence on their part are understandable and need to be acknowledged. Empathy with Welsh or Scottish national aspirations is rooted in sensitivity to the history of subjugation of these two nations by the English and a subsequent recognition of the need to acknowledge their desires. It is also rooted in a sense that over-centralization had created the impetus for devolution. Above all this involves an abandonment of the notion of English supremacy and recognition of the value of the 'Celtic fringe' in its contribution to cultural life. One of the women we interviewed, for example, said:[2]

I've come to realise that to say that I'm English is somehow offensive to people in Scotland and Wales. I think I didn't properly recognise the degree to which there was a sense of resentment against English supremacist approaches.

The 1997 Labour's government's implementation of devolution might partly have reflected the new presence of women inside the party's hierarchy and support among women members of the electorate. Labour introduced a quota system designed to increase its number of women MPs and a raft of policies aimed at attracting women voters.

Also, in direct contrast to traditional Englishness that defined itself in opposition to cosmopolitanism (namely, through anti-European sentiment), this new Englishness is *cosmopolitan* in the sense that it rejects the notion that European integration is somehow threatening and that Britain runs the risk of being overwhelmed by 'jack-booted' Germans. It enjoys the coexistence of different cultures and languages, and values being able to borrow aspects of other cultures. The women interviewed for this research also showed tolerance for other cultures, including support for closer integration into Europe and for minority cultures within the British state. All but one of the women we spoke to expressed some kind of identification with Europe, although few would have described themselves as European when asked about their national identity. They felt an affinity with Europe for political, historical and cultural reasons. In particular, they thought that Britain shared with other European countries a tradition of social democracy and liberalism. As one woman said:

I very strongly identify with Europe. I think it means understanding that our history is a European history. [There is a] wonderful book by Norman Davies that describes all of our kings, for a long way through our history, using their foreign names. They were foreign, they spoke foreign languages. We were utterly integrated with Europe. Our history is the story of Europe, whether it's the story of Protestantism or anything else. Our cultural history is European. That's where we belong. We don't belong in America. America is interesting, but other. Our traditions, our ways of thinking, a lot of our history and experience is deeply bound up with Europe. Our aspirations. *We are all moderate, essentially social democratic nations and we have the same sort of tradition of growing slowly through liberalism to becoming more liberal and more tolerant.*

(emphasis added)

Women are 'declassed' more quickly and extensively than men when economies and societies become post-industrial; middle-class women (still defined often by their male partner's occupation) develop social democratic, internationalist, radical and cosmopolitan views more readily than middle-class men.

This new Englishness is also cosmopolitan in the sense that it welcomes rather than fears multiculturalism. It does not resent expressions of a multicultural and multi-faith country in the form of, for example, the growth of mosques. It celebrates cultural diversity and heterogeneity. All of the women interviewed were cosmopolitan in their approach to other cultures and actively promoted the need for tolerance of cultural diversity and objected to traditional expressions of English identity as xenophobic and illiberal. For example, when asked to describe what she saw as typical traits of Englishness and whether she identified with them one woman said 'Well . . . warm beer and cricket . . . No, not at all' and 'I like living in a complex, multicultural city'. Having dissociated herself from her father's middle Englandness, she said 'I support tolerance and variety and openness, rather than what I see as a closed culture'. Another said:

> The sense of it (national identity) is probably very strong. But it doesn't mean that one should include in that sense any feeling of separateness from other strong identities. I may be aware of the colour of my skin – but that obviously doesn't mean that 'it's better than anything else'. It would be as ludicrous as saying that because I can't help being aware I've got red hair, for instance, it means I should go around joining up with other people with red hair, saying that we're going to fight people with blond hair. It's not the same feeling as that. It's a strong sense of it, but not in any way as being different or better or worthier, or anything else.

Whereas traditional Englishness was earnest in its belief in a pure English national identity, these women have a sense of irony about their national identity, an awareness that English identity has never been pure and impervious to other cultures, and a recognition that the notion of a pure English identity is compromised by the fact that, historically, it borrowed from Celtic ideas of Britishness and Welsh legends such as that of King Arthur (see Langlands 1999: 60). This way of thinking acknowledges the relatively recent consolidation of the nation state and the view that people who live in England did not always think of themselves as 'English' or subscribe to a view that the nation was worth sacrificing one's life for (see Billig 1995: 20–1). We also found some scepticism or distance from national identity and an awareness of its historical contingency. These women all shared this kind of approach to national identity, partly because they were conscious of how their own sense of identity had changed.

One of those interviewed argued that there was no such thing as a pure nation and that any national population contained within it elements of other nationalities:

> I'm very aware of how utterly mixed we all are . . . There isn't such a thing as pure Englishness. There isn't such as thing as pure Welsh either. We're all very mixed. With a huge amount of migration in all directions, and all coming from different places. There's always been a tradition of waves of migration and I defy anybody to prove them-selves to be pure English for many generations.

Whereas traditional Englishness included a significant masculinist culture, these women are espousing a sense of English identity which is 'feminine' in its empathy with different cultures and which opposes the formation of hostile camps and tendencies towards warfare on nationalist grounds. It is not necessarily pacifistic in so far as it supports war in certain circumstances. However, support for war is couched in universalistic principles and human rights agendas rather than particularistic national-ist ideals. While the 'insider/outsider' dichotomy continues to have pur-chase, being on the outside is not portrayed as negative.

There was general opposition to militaristic expressions of national identity and, rather, an empathy for other cultures. All of the women inter-viewed openly expressed either hostility to militarism or a 'sadness' about it. When discussing the Falklands war, none of them celebrated it or felt exalted by it or said that it gave them a sense of pride in the national identity. On the contrary, the women interviewed found the conflict alien-ating and 'embarrassing':

> I certainly have a horror of any patriotic flag-waving jingoistic aware-ness of being English. God forbid! No, I don't think so. Things like the Falklands war, if anything, made me feel very confused about the whole business of how one should behave in the world now.

And another said:

> I was embarrassed to be – I was going to say British – during the Falklands war – I think it's also part of having been involved in politics for many years – part of it is seeing yourself as part of an over-all political or ideological movement. So the issue of national identity is a bit fuzzy for me.

These women are espousing a forward-looking *creative* national identity – they are actively promoting a break with traditional Englishness in their rejection of supremacist attitudes and in their celebration of cultural diversity, Europeanness and expressions of Welsh and Scottish cultural and/or national aspirations. The reasons why we have called these women's views an expression of cosmopolitan or benign Englishness rather than anti-nationalist is because a sense of national identity need not be incompatible with internationalist principles. Although there is a current of thinking that globalism and localism and cosmopolitanism and nationalism are two extremes, it may be that a position is emerging that is both cosmopolitan and sensitive to benign expressions of local identity and multiculturalism.

The 'break-up of Britain' offers scope for the transformation of identities. In this context, some key minority representatives of the elite who grew up in Britain in the post-war period are offering positive narratives and seeking to shape the public agenda on nationalism and national identity in the new historical/political context. These narratives are cosmopolitan in their adoption of identities that transcend national boundaries, such as 'global citizen'. However, such universalist concepts are being combined with tolerance for benign local and national identities.

Conclusion

We have argued that active generations make a generative contribution to a political culture rather than passively accepting it. Active generations, formed in response to traumatic events such as warfare, also tend to play a part in shaping the national consciousness of their generation. In the past, the intellectuals contributing to this have tended to be men, leading to the creation of patriarchal nationalism on an almost universal basis. In discussing nationalism and women, feminist theory has neglected the relationship between gender and generations and failed therefore to explore the role of women as an active generation in creating new political and national cultures.

We would suggest that there is no necessary connection between nationalism and masculinity and once women are in a position to shape nationalist ideas there are openings for transforming past nationalist conceptions. The same traumatic events that arouse (or reorient) national feeling also tend to empower women – for example, women took an enhanced economic role running factories in the First and Second World Wars (and participation rate was ratcheted up). They also took over as dynastic rulers, for example in India, Pakistan, Bangladesh when violent acts killed the father figure. Thus, there is a common stimulus to reorientation and formation of national consciousness.

The symbols of Britishness/Englishness that have declined in the post-war period have all been male – the factory-based workshop of the world; colonies; cricket; football teams and parliament. When discussing British national decline it is masculine themes and practices that are being talked about. Although British/English nationalism has traditionally contained significant masculine currents, there are signs that a new national consciousness is being constructed that is less masculine and more feminine and cosmopolitan. The shift from a warfare state to a welfare state (post-war) is a shift from a national inclination that fulfils male desires to a national institution that fulfils female desires: state-provided welfare gives women resources and opportunities which were only previously achievable by trade unions, mutual aid societies and other private non-capitalist institutions whose membership comprised (and where benefits flowed to) almost exclusively men.

While it would be simplistic to claim that 1960s women, with backgrounds in CND and the anti-war and racism protests, have caused this shift, it is plausible to suggest that they have contributed to setting a new agenda and introducing a benign nationalism in a context when warfare (at least equivalent to the two world wars) has become a very remote possibility. It is difficult to delineate the impact of women's opposition to exclusive, narrow and masculine forms of nationalism on wider national consciousness. However, there is evidence of a broader departure from traditional conceptions of British and English national identities. The women's peace movement in Greenham Common, although widely ridiculed by elements of the popular media at the time, does seem to have been important in reforming consciousness of militarism (see Roseneil 1995). Contemporary political commentators such as Andrew Marr have started to argue against traditional forms of British or English nationalism. The Labour Party too has begun promoting a nationalism that seeks to reinvent itself rather than hark back to the distant past. Moreover, if one assumes a 'trickle-down' model of ideological change, there may be grounds for believing that these ideas could become more widespread.

The traumatic events that made these women into a politically active and conscious generation were those of the 1960s – the decline of the commonwealth, post-war decolonization, movements for national liberation, the Vietnam war, anti-racism and anti-colonialism. While British women were passive in that they were remotely related to the 'hot' wars of the era, their vicarious experience of these and their involvement in the protests against, for example, the Vietnam war and apartheid were formative for them. This was because it was during this time that movements and protests became global in an unprecedented way. Despite the divisions that existed between socialism and feminism and the ensuing arguments about the relative priorities of class and gender, important alliances emerged in the sixties and seventies between socialism and feminism that were mutually influential. The anti-militaristic orientation of the women's movement clearly had an impact on intellectual thought.

Women have become more influential as a result of 1960s educational reforms that brought women into universities in great numbers. These women are influential as a generation because they are highly educated. They benefited from the opportunities provided by post-war affluence and the expansion of education, enabling them to partake more closely in the public sphere. These conditions provided them with the resources to influence the current debates over national identity in the post-British context and to imagine a national identity that is less masculine and more feminine and cosmopolitan. The postwar generation of women is an active generation in the sense that it has both benefited from the opportunities of a particular era and used its public position to influence cultural and political ideas.

Abstracting from this particular case, there are possibilities for asking questions and providing some provisional answers about the more general issue of the conditions that promote cosmopolitan nationalism. One possible clue to the answer lies in the peculiarity of the English case. For centuries, Britain has been unique in Europe in the extent of stability it has experienced and in the reformist character of change it has undergone. Unlike some of its European counterparts, Britain did not endure so-called 'second revolutions' that involved dramatic challenges to the state. Ever since the late seventeenth century, change in Britain developed gradually: 'No "gale of creative destruction" had blown through the creaking political timbers of the United Kingdom for nearly three centuries when the victorious powers met at Potsdam' (Anderson 1992: 155–6). Unlike France and Spain, it was not occupied during the Second World War and did not therefore experience fascism at first hand or the resistance movements.

It seems that the extreme masculinist types of nationalism are particularly evident in situations of heightened turmoil. The use of feminine symbols of the nation vary in different historical contexts and spaces and became more important in times of war and upheaval. For example, the use of Britannia as a national symbol waxed and waned – after centuries of absence, she became very important at the time of Nelson's death (Dresser 1989). Masculinist nationalism becomes far more prominent in situations where there is heightened conflict with the 'other'. In contrast, and despite increasingly vocal demands on the part of the 'Celtic fringe' for separation and the sharpening up of internal boundaries, there is no overwhelming threat to the English from an external 'other'.

There seems to be a connection between older nations, feeling secure in their sense of community, being less aggressive than newly constructed nations. English nationalism evolved gradually rather than radically. In contrast, Britishness was constructed through warfare, making it more masculine, and this is where the idea of founding fathers seems to have particular purchase. However, later generations of migrants challenged this construction along with the new generation of women. In the contemporary context, as devolution is taking place, there are no seismic developments, no dramatic 'break-up' of the United Kingdom (Nairn 2000). Now that England and Britain are faced with having to be reconstructed in a context where warfare on a worldwide scale seems unlikely, it is possible that evolutionary Britain or devolved England could adopt female symbols. Labour's adoption of the rose as an icon seems suggestive of this.

It is possible therefore that particularly masculine forms of nationalism in Britain are declining as the traumatic events of 1914 and 1945 lose their social force. The idea of Europe is no longer threatening. Notwithstanding the standpoint of the Conservative right, much of the rivalry between Britain and its European partners tends to be fairly benign and centres largely on economic issues such as the beef crisis and currency – even though crises such as these can lead to the surfacing of mutual stereotyping in the popular press. Moreover, there is strong recognition of the shared nature of historical experiences and wartime alliances as well as the shared commitment to parliamentary democracy. There are no grounds for fear of anything more sinister than economic competition. This enables opinion makers safely to promote European identity without unduly alienating the general public. Moreover, the European Union has special significance for women, because in areas that directly affect women it stands for progressive values and policies (see Walby 1992).

Moreover, the upper and middle classes have become more international and global. The elite is centrally involved in the globalizing processes taking place. The global economy is to some extent undermining the nation state and, it is sometimes suggested, we are entering a 'borderless world' (Axford 1995: 30). An implication of this is that nationalist feeling and identity are evolving. While national identity is not becoming redundant, there is potential for its character to become more cosmopolitan and open. In his discussion of utopia, Mannheim ([1952] 1997a) claimed that it was the rising classes and not the declining classes that promoted utopian ideals. Taking this theme and applying it to generations, it is possible that it is the generation that is going along with historical changes such as globalization that is promoting constructive, cosmopolitan national identities, whereas the generations that are resisting these changes are espousing reactive nationalism.

Notes

1 It is acknowledged that the public/private dichotomy may not be universally applicable and might have more analytical purchase in western countries.
2 The following unattributed quotations come from interviews carried out in 1999/2000 for our research on elite women and national identity (Edmunds and Turner 2001).

CHAPTER 6

Conclusion

When Karl Mannheim ([1952] 1997a), working in Germany between 1920 and 1933, wrote his essay on generations, he could scarcely have imagined the ways in which, at the conclusion of the twentieth century and in the first part of the twenty-first century, generations could share a consciousness that transcends national boundaries. Mannheim wrote about specific generations that existed in a national context such as the generation of conservative Romantics in Germany in the nineteenth century. Global communication is creating global generations. Nowhere is this more clearly illustrated than in the international response to the terrorist attack on the World Trade Center in New York. When the French President declared that 'We are all Americans', he might have equally observed that we are now a generation that is defined by 11 September 2001. Described by the media as 'Doomsday', this event will be critical in defining future generations, shaking the foundations of generation X. It is an especially poignant illustration of a new global generation, brought into being through developments that go back to the 1960s. While it is New Yorkers that were most affected by this experience, the people who worked inside the building came from right across the world. Moreover, their work was the epitome of globalization in that it involved the management of the world economy and international finance. Ironically too it was globalization that helped to create worldwide terrorist networks with the resources by which they could carry out their anti-globalization attacks. The collapse of the World Trade Center was a tragic confirmation of the view expressed prophetically by Benjamin Barber (1995) that the world is organized around the dialectic of Jihad versus McWorld, between local anti-global loyalties and the neutral cosmopolitanism of world trade. While these developments might well undermine the more positive outcomes of globalization, such as the cosmopolitanism that we have discussed in this book, it seems more likely that it will create a generation that will seek to end the possibilities of similar horrors in the future. Already, political narratives are talking about its impact on future generations in much the same way as Hiroshima generated a 'never again' movement.

This event highlights the need for sociology to address the role of generations in social life and cultural and political change and to abandon its traditional preoccupations. Although experience and memory of this catastrophe will be mediated by other factors, especially perhaps religious, it nevertheless brings into sharp relief the role of traumatic events in creating generational consciousness, in this case, a generational consciousness that is global.

There are other reasons why sociology needs to explore further the value of generation as an analytical category. First, there is mounting evidence that the post-war generation, by virtue of its size and its strategic position, has been particularly critical to social change in the twentieth century. Second, the post-war generation has also been important to the rise of modern consumerism which tends to be structured around generational markets – motivated largely by the creation of a youth movement that, far more than social class, seems to shape contemporary fashion. Third, the demographic changes associated with the growth of an ageing population have created a range of pressing social policy issues and increased potential for intergenerational conflict. Governments have been forced to grapple with welfare issues turning on state dependency and heightened intergenerational conflict because of issues surrounding scarce resources as well as political developments such as the emergence of the 'grey vote'. The global crisis that has been reinforced by the terrorist attacks of September 2001 has underlined the social and economic problems of pension funds, life insurance and superannuation that are closely related to the retirement of the ageing baby boomers.

Now that the sociological analysis of social class has become increasingly a sterile area of research, the time seems particularly ripe for sociological and historical innovation in research on generations. The existing literature on generations has been both insightful and productive in terms of discrete empirical studies. However, since the time Mannheim published his essay on generations in 1928 and 1929, there has been little theoretical development in sociological thinking on generations. In this book we have provided a sociology of generations that develops the classical approach to generations offered by Mannheim by complementing it with the cultural sociology of Pierre Bourdieu (1988, 1993a). Bourdieu has introduced a range of concepts that can be applied to understanding how generations contribute to social, cultural and political change.

Mannheim's initial insight provides a basic understanding of how generational consciousness emerges, namely through the shared experience of a traumatic historical event. Generational consciousness, following Halbwachs (1992), is then sustained and reinforced through collective memories and rituals. However, neither of these accounts provides an explanation of how generations and generational consciousness might act to affect various changes. Bourdieu's specific contribution to the study of generations and social change, especially in the cultural field, has generally been ignored. Its explanatory value resides in the way that it draws attention to the role of intergenerational conflict in bringing about social transformation, where cultural change takes place in a given field through competition over scarce resources between generations. Thus, the social success of emerging generations takes place through competition with their predecessors, that is with existing generations in power. The sociology of generations is essentially a sociology of social change, conceptualized as the endless, but often implicit, struggle over cultural influence.

Having distinguished in this book between two definitions of generation, one chronological and the other social, we suggest that the chronological understanding of generation is not sociologically interesting or fruitful. This understanding of generation cannot shed light on the formation of generational cultures and politics or the way that given generations may attract different age groups. It is quite possible for the culture and politics developed within a particular generational cohort to become attractive to groups that do not, in a chronological sense, belong to that generation. Using an analogy with class and the way members of one class may be attracted to the politics of another, it is also the case that people who were born in the 1980s may identify with the politics of the 1960s. Nor does a chronological understanding of generation shed light on how a generational consciousness produced in one era can continue to operate in another. It is hence more appropriate to call a 'chronological generation' a 'cohort'. This study has been concerned to understand how cohorts become generations through acquiring a collective consciousness or memory, especially a political consciousness of the long-term effects of traumatic events. The New York attacks will create a 'September generation' that will be conscious of the negative effects of terrorism on their life chances (for travel, urban security, global employment, civil liberties, national identity and relationship to religious movements and the third world), thereby dividing them from baby boomers who experienced the global world, especially after the Cold War, as an open space.

We argue that a distinction between active and passive generations is useful because it takes account of this strategic component of generations, illuminating the process by which generations overhaul pre-existing forms of thinking or doing. While a generation might be formed in response to a traumatic event such as war, it becomes a strategic, acting generation by exploiting available resources to innovate in the cultural, intellectual or political spheres. We suggest further that it is interesting to conceptualize generations as alternating between active and passive generations. Thus an active generation that transforms social and cultural life tends to be followed by a passive one that simply inherits the changes wrought by its more successful predecessor. Successful generations, especially large generations, create the conditions and set the terms of action for their successors. Contemporary British history can partly be understood in terms of a fluctuation between active and passive generations, that is, an active wartime generation was followed by a passive inter-war generation, which was followed by an active consumer generation, which in turn was followed by a passive generation X. The active sixties generation set up the liberal institutions inherited by its successors who, by virtue of this political heritage, became politically apathetic. Their apathy reflected the fact that there remained little for them to protest against. New issues continued to be defined in terms of the legacy of the 1960s.

There is reason to suppose that the 1960s generation provided the initial impulse towards globalization. The booming economies of the post-war period, the reduction in the costs of transport and communication, the creation of worldwide labour markets and the arrival of the Internet have provided the material conditions of cultural globalization. This 1960s generation was the first truly global one, expressed in the invention of the concept of a 'global village' (McLuhan 1968). Global television gave people access to information in an unprecedented way. By the 1990s, global forms of communication, including the telephone, e-mail and the Internet, enabled people to act on that information. In McLuhan's terms, television was a 'cold' medium because viewers were reactive/passive. In contrast the new media are 'hot' because they allow users to be proactive and participative. There is a strong historical connection between the growth of postmodern culture, global communications, innovative consumer lifestyles and the post-war generation.

It could therefore be argued that the globalization of culture is itself the product of the 1960s generation. The political protests and cultural innovations and challenges to social conventions that began during this decade have, we suggest, had a profound impact on the global landscape. The cultural impact of this generation follows from the fact that this generation was unique in the breadth of its influence, with social movements spreading across the US, Australia, Scandinavia and western Europe. As we have shown, these generational movements had a specific set of consequences for the status of women and minorities in geographically disparate areas. It was this generation that was the first to make effective use of information technologies that ushered in a new global era. The specific challenge for new generations is whether the New York attacks will bring in a period of nationalist anti-globalization that will close off these cultural opportunities for an active generation.

At the start of the new millennium, there has been considerable nostalgia and introspection about the 1960s in an attempt to evaluate the cultural and social impact of the post-war generation that has now reached maturity. Critics such as Bloom (1987) have argued that the democratization of culture has led to its dumbing down and that an extreme form of relativism has undermined standards and created potential for conflict between social groups. While accepting some of the criticisms of this decade, we argue that on balance the impact of the 1960s has been broadly beneficial. Its internationalism created the conditions for a new range of interconnections between different cultures, laying the foundation for greater tolerance of cultural diversity, for entrepreneurial innovation and opportunities for women. Indeed, it seems that the 1960s was a major impulse in the creation of intellectual generations of women who were able, in many cases for the first time, to enter higher education *en masse* and who were politicized by the events of this decade.

Our main concern then has been to show that generations rather than classes have shaped contemporary cultural, intellectual and political thought. In contrast to traditional sociological understanding of intellectual development as rooted in specific economic circumstances, we suggest that intellectuals are determined not by class but by generational location and the effect of generational experiences. Thus we argue against the traditional sociological view of intellectuals as being shaped primarily by their class location, and illustrate the greater effect of generational experience. Moreover, war, occupation and migration seem to have been especially important in creating those active intellectual generations that have been the carriers of major cultural innovations. This understanding of the connections between generational consciousness and intellectual change means that the history of ideas that has emphasized class or institutions (academics or universities) rather than generations is inadequate. Moreover, because generations rather than classes shaped the construction of knowledge, Mannheim's view of intellectuals acting independently of economic interests is more sociologically relevant than the legacy of Marxism that has ignored the specific effects of traumatic events on historical consciousness via the formation of generations out of cohorts.

Drawing on Mannheim's ([1936] 1997b) distinction between forward-looking and backward-looking groups in his analysis of conservatism, we make a distinction between nostalgic and utopian intellectual generations – intellectuals are important in expressing either utopian (forward-looking) or nostalgic (backward-looking) visions. Utopian intellectuals introduce ideas that aim to change the status quo whereas nostalgic intellectuals promote ideas that hark back to the past and tend to preserve the status quo. Through a discussion of intellectual generations including the Frankfurt School, the New York Intellectuals, French intellectuals and diasporic intellectuals such as Edward Said, we suggest that, ironically, creative intellectuals of the second part of the twentieth century turned towards social conservatism as a result of the insecurity generated by their generational experiences of rootlessness. Ultimately the rootless intellectual contributes to the erosion of national barriers and the creation of the global, cosmopolitan intellectual. The creation of the Internet has contributed to the contradictory role of intellectuals as carriers of national cultures through their embedded role in national academic institutions and as carriers of cosmopolitan cultures that corrode national boundaries. Intellectuals are particularly exposed to the contradictory dialectic of Jihad and McWorld.

This book also departs from traditional sociology in the way it seeks to link generations with the creation and re-creation of nationalist consciousness. Although the study of nationalism recently has become a strong area of sociological thought, it has neglected the contribution of generational change and experience on nationalism in the face of historical evidence that suggests a close connection (Braungart 1984). Our theory is that the traumatic events that create generations also generate national consciousness, which is articulated by intellectual generations. At the point of a nation's creation, these intellectuals contribute culturally to the creation of the founding fathers. Traumatic events are critical to the formation of active generations and generational consciousness. In turn, these active generations, through intellectual articulation, play an important role in shaping national consciousness.

Founding fathers take on a particularly important role in the construction of newer nations (such as the US or Israel or Pakistan) than in the evolution of ancient nations (such as France and England). In the former, which is originally based on civic values, the invented and imposed unity has weak foundations because the nation is based on formerly disparate groups. This political context means that the founding fathers have to create a primordial sense of belonging which contrasts with the original inclusive impetus. They tend to do this by creating a national image that denies diversity and therefore marginalizes certain groups. Generations of founding fathers have constructed nations that have been largely patriarchal, headed by 'dominant' father figures. Good examples of this include Kemal Attaturk in relation to the creation of Turkey, Jinnah in relation to modern Pakistan and Napoleon Bonaparte in relation to modern France. However, as migration starts to take a hold, the need to widen out and deconstruct the supposed primordial character of the nation becomes pressing. Newer generations of migrants therefore play an important part in deconstructing primordial versions of national identity in favour of more open versions.

Traditional feminist theory has also neglected generation as an important variable. We suggest that the literature on women and nationalism needs to take account of the role of generations of women in re-creating national consciousness. Founding nationalist narratives have generally excluded women, apart from having them as figureheads (in caring/nurturing or sexual roles). The image of the suffering of women is often employed as an image of national suffering as in the case of Joan of Arc or the vulnerable woman in Eugene Delacroix's 'La Grèce sur les ruines de Missolonghi'. Gender is therefore important because of the way women have been marginalized in these narratives or else stereotyped. However, we would argue that newer generations of women, themselves created out of traumatic events such as the First and Second World Wars, Algeria and Vietnam, have been critical to opposing aggressive forms of nationalism and that the 1960s generation in particular, having gained access to the public realm and internationalized by developments in the 1960s, are now in a position to construct less aggressive models and benign nationalism. Feminist theory therefore needs to divert some of its attention on ethnicity and class to the crucial role of generational consciousness.

Perhaps one of the salient conclusions of sociological research in the last thirty years has been that personal identities have been fragmented by rapid social change. These new forms of flexible identity have often been associated with the decline of social class and the transformation of work by casualization and new information technology. Sociologists have spoken about the 'corrosion of character' (Sennett 1998). There is a sense in which the idiom of class has been replaced by a sense of the fragility and fragmentation of identity in society. These changes are often seen within the broader context of post-industrialism or postmodernism. However, our argument is that these accounts of identity and social change have neglected a powerful and enduring feature of modern identity, namely generation. We have explored how this aspect of identity and consciousness has been fundamental in shaping national identity, intellectual cultures and global awareness. Generational identity through the twentieth century was fundamental in shaping national consciousness. The political awareness of young Palestinians is a generational consciousness of the Intifada, and the political awareness of the youth of New York is a product of the attack on the WTO towers. Thus, the traumatic events of the start of the new millennium demonstrate that generation will continue to be a foundation of modern politics, culture and consciousness.

Bibliography

Adorno, T. W., Frenkel-Brunswick, E., Levinson, D. J. and Sanford, R. N. (1950) *The Authoritarian Personality*. New York, NY: Harper.

Adorno, T. W. and Horkheimer, M. ([1944] 1979) *Dialectic of Enlightenment*. London: Verso.

Ahmed, A. S. (1992) *Postmodernism and Islam, Predicament and Promise*. London and New York, NY: Routledge.

Alexander, P. (1995) *James Dean: Boulevard of Broken Dreams*. London: Warner Books.

Allen, H. (2000) Gender, sexuality and the military model of US national community, in T. Mayer (ed) *Gender Ironies of Nationalism: Sexing the Nation*, pp. 309–28. London and New York, NY: Routledge.

Anderson, B. (1983) *Imagined Communities*. London: Verso.

Anderson, C. (1993) *Jagger Unauthorized*. New York, NY: Delacorte Press.

Anderson, P. (1992) *English Questions*. London and New York, NY: Verso.

Anderson, T. H. (1995) *The Movement and the Sixties*. New York, NY and Oxford: Oxford University Press.

Anthias, F. and Yuval-Davis, N. (1989) Introduction, in N. Yuval-Davis and F. Anthias, *Woman–Nation–State*. Houndsmills, Basingstoke and London: Macmillan Press.

Asad, T. (1993) *Genealogies of Religion*. Baltimore, MD and London: Johns Hopkins University Press.

Austen, J. ([1814] 1996) *Mansfield Park*. London: Penguin.

Axford, B. (1995) *The Global System, Economics, Politics and Culture*. Cambridge: Polity Press.

Barber, B. R. (1995) *Jihad vs McWorld. How Globalism and Tribalism are Re-shaping the World*. New York, NY: Ballantine Books.

Barker, E. (1995) The post-war generation and establishment religion in England, in W. C. Roof, W. C. Jackson and D. A Roozen (eds) *The Post-War Generation and Establishment Religion, Cross Cultural Perspectives*, pp. 1–25. Boulder, CO, San Francisco, CA: Oxford.

Baudelot, C. and Establet, R. (1998) *Thirty Years Old in 1968 and 1998*. Paris: PUF.

Baudrillard, J. (1983) *Simulations*. New York, NY: Semiotext(e).

Baudrillard, J. (1988) *America*. London: Verso.

Bell, D. ([1967] 1996) *Marxian Socialism in the United States*. Ithaca, NY, London: Cornell University Press.

Bell, D. (1980) *Sociological Journeys: Essays 1960–1980*. London: Heinemann.

Bellah, R. (1975) *The Broken Covenant. American Civil Religion in a Time of Trial*. New York, NY: Seabury Press.

Berg, A. S. (1981) *Max Perkins: Editor of Genius*. London: Macdonald Futura.

Berger, P. L. and Luckmann, T. (1966) *The Social Construction of Reality. A Treatise in the Sociology of Knowledge*. London: Allen Lane.

Bhattacharyya, G. (1999) Teaching race in cultural studies: a ten-step programme of personal development in M. Bulmer and J. Solomos (eds) *Ethnic and Racial Studies Today*, pp. 73–84. London and New York, NY: Routledge.

Bigsby, C. W. E. (ed.) (1975) *Superculture: American Popular Culture and Europe*. London: Paul Elek.

Billig, M. (1995) *Banal Nationalism*. London, Thousand Oaks, New Delhi: Sage Publications.

Bloom, A. (1986) *Prodigal Sons: The New York Intellectuals and their World*. Oxford: Oxford University Press.

Bloom, A. (1987) *The Closing of the American Mind*. New York, NY: Simon and Schuster.

Bloom, A. (1993) *Love and Friendship*. New York, NY: Simon and Schuster.

Blum, J. M. (1991) *Years of Discord: American Politics and Society 1961–1974*. New York, NY: Norton.

Boesche, R. (1988) Why did Tocqueville fear abundance? Or the tension between commerce and citizenship, *History of European Ideas*, 9(1): 25–45.

Bourdieu, P. (1984) *Distinction. A Social Critique of the Judgement of Taste*. London: Routledge.

Bourdieu, P. (1988) *Homo Academicus*. Stanford: Stanford University Press.

Bourdieu, P. (1990a) *The Logic of Practice*. Cambridge: Polity Press.

Bourdieu, P. (1990b) *In Other Words: Essays Towards Reflexive Sociology*. Cambridge: Polity Press.

Bourdieu, P. (1993a) 'Youth' is just a word, in *Sociology in Question*, pp. 94–102. London: Sage.

Bourdieu, P. (1993b) *The Field of Cultural Production: Essays on Art and Literature.* Cambridge: Polity Press.

Bourdieu, P. (1996) *The Rules of Art.* Cambridge: Polity Press.

Bourdieu, P. and Passeron, J. C. (1990) *Reproduction in Education, Society and Culture.* London: Sage.

Braungart, R. G. (1984) Historical generations and generation units: a global pattern of youth movements, *Journal of Political and Military Society*, 12: 113–35.

Braungart, R. G. and Braungart, M. M. (1986) Life-course and generational politics, *Annual Review of Sociology*, 12: 205–31.

Brogan, H. (1985) *Longman History of the United States of America.* London: Longman.

Buckley, W. and Seaton, J. (eds) (1992) *Beyond Cheering and Bashing: New Perspectives on* The Closing of the American Mind. Bowling Green, OH: Bowling Green State University Press.

Bude, H. (1995) *Das Altern einer Generation. Die Jahrgange 1938–1948.* Frankfurt am Main: Suhrkamp.

Burner, D. (1996) *Making Peace with the 60s.* Princeton, NJ: Princeton University Press.

Caine, B. (1997) *English Feminism, 1780–1980.* Oxford: Oxford University Press.

Calhoun, C. (1998) Social theory and the public space, in B. S. Turner (ed.) *The Blackwell Companion to Social Theory*, pp. 429–70. Oxford: Blackwell Publishers.

Camus, A. ([1948] 1998) *The Plague*, trans. S. Gilbert. London: Penguin.

Camus, A. (1983) *The Outsider*, trans. J. Laredo. London: Penguin.

Caute, D. (1988) *Sixty-Eight, the Year of the Barricades.* London: Paladin Books.

Centre for Contemporary Cultural Studies (1982) *The Empire Strikes Back: Race and Racism in 70s Britain.* London: Hutchinson/Birmingham: CCCS.

Chaney, D. (1996) *Lifestyles.* London: Routledge.

Charters, A. (1992) *The Portable Beat Reader.* New York, NY: Penguin.

Chauvel, L. (1998) *The Destiny of Generations: Social Structures and Cohorts in 20th Century France.* Paris: PUF.

Chen, K.-H. (1996) The formation of a diasporic intellectual. An interview with Stuart Hall, in D. Morley and Kuan-Hsing Chen (eds) *Stuart Hall: Critical Dialogues in Cultural Studies*, pp. 484–503. London and New York, NY: Routledge.

Cohen, S. (1972) *Folk Devils and Moral Panics.* London: Paladin.

Coleman, J. (1990) *Foundations of Social Theory.* Cambridge, MA: The Belknap Press.

Colley, L. (1996) *Britons Forging the Nation, 1707–1837.* London: Vintage.

Collier, P. and Horowitz, D. (1989) *Destructive Generation: Second Thoughts About the Sixties.* New York, NY: Summit Books.

Collins, R. (1998) *The Sociology of Philosophies: A Global Theory of Intellectual Change.* Cambridge, MA and London: Harvard University Press.

Connelly, R. (ed.) (1995) *In The Sixties: The Writing that Captured a Decade.* London: Pavilion.

Connerton, P. (1989) *How Societies Remember*. Cambridge: Cambridge University Press.

Coombs, A. (1996) *Sex and Anarchy: The Life and Death of the Sydney Push*. New York, NY: Viking.

Corse, S. M. (1997) *Nationalism and Literature: The Politics of Culture in Canada and the United States*. Cambridge: Cambridge University Press.

Corsten, M. (1999) The time of generations, *Time and Society*, 8(2): 249–72.

Dahrendorf, R. (1982) *On Britain*. London: BBC.

Davies, H. (1987) *Sartre and* Les Temps Modernes. Cambridge: Cambridge University Press.

Davis, M. (1997) *Gangland: Cultural Elites and the New Generationalism*. St Leonards: Allen & Unwin.

de Beauvoir, S. ([1953] 1997) *The Second Sex*, trans. H. M. Parschley. London: Vintage.

de Beauvoir, S. (1984) *Adieux: A Farewell to Sartre*. Harmondsworth: Penguin Books.

Dennis, N., Henriques, F. M. and Slaughter, C. (1962) *Coal is Our Life*. London: Eyre and Spottiswoode.

Diggins, J. P. (1994) *The Promise of Pragmatism: Modernism and the Crisis of Knowledge and Authority*. Chicago, IL and London: University of Chicago Press.

Dobson, A. (1993) *Jean-Paul Sartre and the Politics of Reason: A Theory of History*. Cambridge: Cambridge University Press.

Dodd, P. (1995) *The Battle Over Britain*. London: Demos.

Dresser, M. (1989) Britannia in R. Samuel (ed.) *Patriotism: The Making and Unmaking of British National Identity. Volume III: National Fictions*. London: Routledge.

Drury, S. B. (1997) *Leo Strauss and the American Right*. Basingstoke: Macmillan.

Durkheim, E. (1954) *The Elementary Forms of the Religious Life*. London: Allen & Unwin.

Edmunds, J. (2000) *The Left and Israel. Party Policy Change and Internal Democracy*. Basingstoke and New York, NY: Macmillan.

Edmunds, J. and Turner, B. S. (2001) The re-invention of a national identity? Women and 'cosmopolitan' Englishness, *Ethnicities*, 1(1): 83–108.

Eisenstadt, S. N. (1956) *From Generation to Generation. Age Groups and Social Structure*. New York, NY: Free Press.

Elder, G. H. Jr (1974) *Children of the Great Depression: Social Change in Life Experience*. Chicago, IL: Chicago University Press.

Elder, G. H. Jr and Pellerin, L. A. (1998) Linking history and human lives, in J. Z. Giele and G. H. Elder Jr (eds) *Methods of Life Course Research, Qualitative and Quantitative Approaches*, pp. 264–94. Thousand Oaks, London, New Delhi: Sage Publications.

Eliot, T. S. (1949) *Notes towards the Definition of Culture*. New York, NY: Harcourt Brace.

Eliot, T. S. (1971) *The Waste Land*. London: Faber and Faber.

Enloe, C. (1989) *Bananas, Beaches and Bases: Making Feminist Sense of International Relations*. London: Pandora Press.

Evans, M. (1985) *Simone de Beauvoir: A Feminist Mandarin*. London and New York, NY: Tavistock.

Eyerman, R. (1994) *Between Culture and Politics. Intellectuals in Modern Society*. Cambridge: Polity Press.

Eyerman, R. (2002) Intellectuals and the construction of an African American identity: outline to a generational approach, in J. Edmunds and B. S. Turner (eds) *Generational Consciousness, Narrative and Politics*. Boulder, CO: Rowman and Littlefield.

Eyerman, R. and Jamison, A. (2000) *Music and Social Movements: Mobilizing Traditions in the Twentieth Century*. Cambridge: Cambridge University Press.

Eyerman, R. and Turner, B. S. (1998) Outline of a theory of generations, *European Journal of Social Theory*, 1(1): 91–106.

Farber, D. (ed.) (1994) *The Sixties: From Memory to History*. Chapel Hill and London: University of North Carolina Press.

Featherstone, M., Hepworth, M. and Turner, B. (eds) (1991) *The Body: Social Process and Cultural Theory*. London: Sage.

Foucault, M. (1966) *Les Mots et Les Choses*. Paris: Gallimard.

Fowler, B. (1997) *Pierre Bourdieu and Cultural Theory: Critical Investigations*. London: Sage.

Galbraith, J. K. (1981) *A Life In Our Times: Memoirs*. London: Corgi.

Gellner, E. (1983) *Nations and Nationalism*. Oxford: Basil Blackwell.

Gibson, C. (1993) The four baby boom, *American Demographics*, November: 36–40.

Giele, J. Z. and Elder, G. H. (eds) (1998) *Methods of Life Course Research. Qualitative and Quantitative Approaches*. Thousand Oaks, CA: Sage.

Gilligan, C. (1982) *In A Different Voice: Psychological Theory and Women's Development*. Cambridge, MA and London: Harvard University Press.

Gilroy, P. (1987) *There Ain't No Black in the Union Jack: The Cultural Politics of Race and Nation*. London: Hutchinson.

Gilroy, P. (1997) Diaspora and the detours of identity, in K. Woodward (ed.) *Identity and Difference*, pp. 301–43. London: Sage.

Gilroy, P. (2000) *Between Camps: Nations, Cultures and the Allure of Race*. London and Harmondsworth: Allen Lane, The Penguin Press.

Gilsenan, M. (2000) The education of Edward Said. Review of *Out of Place: A Memoir*, *New Left Review*, 4 (July/August): 152–8.

Ginn, J. and Arber, S. (1995) 'Only connect': gender relations and ageing, in S. Arber and J. Ginn (eds) *Connecting Gender and Ageing*. Buckingham and Philadelphia, PA: Open University Press.

Gitlin, T. (1987) *The Sixties: Years of Hope, Days of Rage*. New York, NY: Bantam.

Glazer, N. (1997) *We Are All Multiculturalists Now*. Cambridge, MA and London: Harvard University Press.

Gramsci, A. (1971) *Selections from the Prison Notebooks*. New York, NY: International Publishers.

Graves, P. (1994) *Labour Women: Women in British Working Class Politics, 1918–1939*. Cambridge: Cambridge University Press.

Greer, G. ([1970] 1981) *The Female Eunuch*. London: MacGibbon & Kee.

Greer, G. (1999) *The Whole Woman*. London: Anchor.

Hagestad, G. O. (1999) A Gray Zone? Meetings between Sociology and Gerontology, *Contemporary Sociology*, 28(5): 14–7.

Halbwachs, M. (1992) *On Collective Memory*. Chicago, IL: University of Chicago Press.

Hall, S. (1992) New ethnicities, in J. Donald and A. Rattansi (eds) *'Race', Culture and Difference*, pp. 252–9. London: Sage Publications/Open University Press.

Hall, S. *et al.* (1978) *Policing the Crisis: Mugging, the State and Law and Order*. Basingstoke: Macmillan Education.

Hassall, C. (1964) *Rupert Brooke: A Biography*. London: Faber and Faber.

Hawthorne, N. ([1850] 1983) *The Scarlet Letter*. London: Penguin.

Hazareesingh, S. (1994) *Political Traditions in Modern France*. Oxford: Oxford University Press.

Hechter, M. (1975) *Internal Colonialism: The Celtic Fringe in British National Development, 1536–1966*. London: Routledge and Kegan Paul.

Heffer, S. (1998) *Like the Roman: The Life of Enoch Powell*. London: Weidenfeld and Nicolson.

Hobsbawm, E. and Ranger, T. (eds) (1988) *The Invention of Tradition*. Cambridge: Cambridge University Press.

Hoggart, R. (1958) *The Uses of Literacy: Aspects of Working-Class Life with Special Reference to Publications and Entertainments*. Harmondsworth: Penguin.

Hoggart, R. (1995) *The Way We Live Now*. London: Pimlico.

Holton, R. and Turner, B. S. (1986) *Talcott Parsons on Economy and Society*. London: Routledge and Kegan Paul.

Howe, I. (1976) *Land of Our Fathers*. New York, NY: Simon and Schuster.

Humm, M. (ed.) (1992) *Feminisms: A Reader*. New York, NY and London: Harvester Wheatsheaf.

Ignatieff, M. (1997) Where are they now? *Prospect*, August–September: 8–9.

Ignatieff, M. (1998) Identity parades, *Prospect*, April, 18–23.

Ignatieff, M. (2000) *Isaiah Berlin: A Life*. London: Vintage.

Isherwood, C. (1996) *Diaries. Volume One: 1939–1960*. London: Methuen.

Jacoby, R. (1987) *The Last Intellectuals*. New York, NY: Basic Books.

Jay, M. (1973) *The Dialectical Imagination: A History of the Frankfurt School and the Institute of Social Research, 1923–1950*. London: Heinemann.

Jay, M. (1986) *Permanent Exiles: Essays on the Intellectual Migration from Germany to America*. New York, NY: Columbia University Press.

Jenkins, R. (1992) *Pierre Bourdieu*. London: Routledge.

Johnson, P. (1997) *A History of the American People*. London: Weidenfeld and Nicolson.

Jones, K. B. (1989) Le mal des fleurs: a feminist response to *The Closing of the American Mind*, *Women and Politics*, 9(4): 1–22.

Jones, M. C. (1992) A Bloom amid the Reagan-bushes, in W. K. Buckley and J. Seaton (eds) *Beyond Cheering and Bashing: New Perspectives on* The Closing of the American Mind, pp. 68–78. Bowling Green, OH: Bowling Green State University Popular Press.

Judt, T. (1992) *Past Imperfect: French Intellectuals, 1944–1956*. Berkeley, CA and Oxford: University of California Press

Kamester, M. and Vellacot, J. (eds) (1987) *Militarism Versus Feminism: Writings on Women and War*. London: Virago.

Kennedy, J. (1995) Building New Babylon: the Netherlands in the sixties. Unpublished PhD thesis, University of Iowa.

Kennedy, J. (1997) *New Babylon and the Politics of Modernity*. Amsterdam: Boom.

Kennedy, L. (1995) *Susan Sontag. Mind as Passion*. Manchester and New York, NY: Manchester University Press.

Kerouac, J. (1958) *On the Road*. New York, NY: Andre Deutsch.

Kertzer, D. E. (1983) Generation as a sociological problem, *Annual Review of Sociology*, 9: 125–49.

King, D. (2000) *Making Americans: Immigration, Race and the Origins of Diverse Democracy*. Cambridge, MA and London: Harvard University Press.

Klatch, R. E. (1999) *A Generation Divided: The New Left, The New Right and the 1960s*. Berkeley, CA, Los Angeles, CA and London: University of California Press.

Koch, A. and Peden, W. (eds) (1944) *The Life and Selected Writings of Thomas Jefferson*. New York, NY: The Modern Library.

Koestler, A. (1940) *Darkness at Noon*. London: Cape.

Kumar, K. (1993) The end of socialism? The end of utopia? The end of history?, in K. Kumar and S. Bann (eds) *Utopias and the Millennium*, pp. 63–80. London: Reaktion Books.

Kumar, K. (2000a) Nation and empire: English and British national identity in comparative perspective, *Theory and Society*, 29: 575–608.

Kumar, K. (2000b) 'Englishness' and English National Identity, in D. Morley and K. Robbins (eds) *British Cultural Studies*. Oxford: Oxford University Press.

Kumar, K. and Bann, S. (eds) (1993) *Utopias and the Millennium*. London: Reaktion Books.

Lagree, J.-C. (1992) From the sociology of youth to the sociology of generations, *Les Sciences de l'Education pour l'Ere Nouvelle*, 3(4): 19–27.

Langlands, R. (1999) Britishness or Englishness? The historical problem of national identity in Britain, *Nations and Nationalism*, 5(1): 53–69.

Lass, A. (1994) From memory to history, in R. S. Watson (ed.) *Memory, History and Opposition Under State Socialism*, pp. 87–104. Santa Fe, New Mexico: School of American Research Press.

Laufer, Robert S. and Bengtson, Vern L. (1974) Generations, aging, and social stratification: on the development of generational units, *Journal of Social Issues*, 30(3): 181–205.

Lauret, M. (1999) 'The approval of Headquarters': race and ethnicity in English studies, in M. Bulmer and J. Solomos (eds) *Ethnic and Racial Studies Today*, pp. 24–35. London: Routledge.

Lee, D. J. (1996) Weak class theories or strong sociology?, in D. J. Lee and B. S. Turner (eds) *Conflicts about Class: Debating Inequality in late Industrialism*, pp. 245–53. London and New York, NY: Longman.

Leslie, E. (1999) Introduction to Adorno/Marcuse correspondence on the German Student Movement, *New Left Review*, 233: 118–23.

Levitas, R. (1986) *The Ideology of the New Right*. Cambridge: Polity.

Light, A. and Chaloupka, W. (2000) Angry white men: right exclusionary nationalism and left identity politics, in T. Mayer (ed.) *Gender Ironies of Nationalism: Sexing the Nation*, pp. 329–50. London and New York, NY: Routledge.

Lipsitz, G. (1994) Youth culture, rock 'n' roll and social crisis, in D. Farber (ed.) *The Sixties: From Memory to History*, pp. 206–34. Chapel Hill, NC and London: University of North Carolina Press.

Longhurst, B. (1989) *Karl Mannheim and the Contemporary Sociology of Knowledge*. Basingstoke: Macmillan.

Lopez, A. (2002) Youth in '90s and youth in '60s Spain: Intergenerational dialogue and struggle, in J. Edmunds and B. S. Turner (eds) *Generational Consciousness, Narrative and Politics*. Boulder, CO: Rowman and Littlefield.

Lovenduski, J. and Randall, V. (1993) *Contemporary Feminist Politics, Women and Power in Britain*. Oxford: Oxford University Press.

McCrone, D. and Kiely, R. (2000) Nationalism and citizenship, *Sociology*, 34(1): 19–34.

McLuhan, M. (1964) *Understanding Media: The Extensions of Man*. Cambridge, MA and London: MIT Press.

McLuhan, M. (1968) *War and Peace in the Global Village*. New York, NY: Bantam.

MacPherson, C. B. (1962) *The Political Theory of Possessive Individualism*. Oxford: Clarendon Press.

Mannheim, K. ([1952] 1997a) The problem of generations, in *Collected Works of Karl Mannheim*, volume 5, pp. 276–320. London: Routledge.

Mannheim, K. ([1936] 1997b) *Ideology and Utopia*. London: Routledge.

Mannheim, K. ([1986] 1997c) *Conservatism: A Contribution to the Sociology of Knowledge*. London: Routledge.

Marcuse, H. ([1955] 1987]) *Eros and Civilization: A Philosophical Inquiry into Freud*. London: Ark.

Martin, A. K. (2000) Death of a nation: transnationalism, bodies and abortion in late twentieth-century Ireland, in T. Mayer (ed.) *Gender Ironies of Nationalism: Sexing the Nation*. London and New York, NY: Routledge.

Marwick, A. (1998) *The Sixties, Cultural Revolution in Britain, France, Italy and the United States c1958–c1974*. Oxford: Oxford University Press.

Matusow, A. J. (1984) *The Unravelling of America: A History of Liberalism in the 1960s*. New York: Harper & Row.

Mayer, K. U. (1988) German survivors of world war II: The impact on the life course of the collective experience of birth cohorts, in M. W. Riley, B. J. Huber and B. B. Hess (eds) *Social Change and the Life Course, Volume I.* Beverly Hills, CA, London and New Delhi: Sage Publications.

Mayer, T. (ed.) (2000a) *Gender Ironies of Nationalism: Sexing the Nation.* London and New York, NY: Routledge.

Mayer, T. (2000b) Gender ironies of nationalism: setting the stage, in T. Mayer (ed.) *Gender Ironies of Nationalism: Sexing the Nation*, pp. 1–24. London and New York, NY: Routledge.

Mayer, T. (2000c) From zero to hero: masculinity in Jewish nationalism, in T. Mayer (ed.) *Gender Ironies of Nationalism: Sexing the Nation*, pp. 283–308. London and New York, NY: Routledge.

Melville, ([1851] 1994) *Moby Dick.* London: Penguin.

Merquior, J. G. (1991) *Foucault.* London: Fontana Press.

Miles, B. (1992) *William Burroughs. El Hombre Invisible.* New York, NY: Virgin Books.

Miller, R. L. (2000) *Researching Life Stories and Family Histories.* London and New Delhi: Sage Publications.

Mitchell, J. (1966) Women: the longest revolution, *New Left Review*, 40: 11–37.

Mitchell, J. (1971) *Woman's Estate.* Harmondsworth: Penguin.

Modood, T. (1994) Political blackness and British Asians, *Sociology*, 28(4): 859–76.

Mol, H. (1985) *The Faith of Australians.* Sydney: George Allen and Unwin.

Moreno, K. and Murphy, M. (1999) Generational warfare, *Forbes*, 163(6): 62–6.

Morley, D. and Chen, K.-H. (eds) (1996) *Stuart Hall: Critical Dialogues in Cultural Studies.* London: Routledge.

Mort, F. (1996) *Cultures of Consumption: Masculinities and Social Space in Late Twentieth-Century Britain.* London and New York, NY: Routledge.

Mosse, G. L. (1985) *Nationalism and Sexuality: Respectability and Abnormal Sexuality in Modern Europe.* New York, NY: H. Fertig.

Mostov, J. (2000) Sexing the nation/desexing the body: politics of national identity in the former Yugoslavia, in T. Mayer (ed.) *Gender Ironies of Nationalism: Sexing the Nation*, pp. 89–112. London and New York, NY: Routledge.

Mulkay, M. J. and Turner, B. S. (1971) Over-production of personnel and innovation in three social settings, *Sociology*, 5(1): 47–61.

Nagel, J. (1998) Masculinity and nationalism: gender and sexuality in the making of nations, *Ethnic and Racial Studies*, 21(2): 242–69.

Nairn, T. (1994) *The Enchanted Glass: Britain and Its Monarchy*, revised edn. London: Vintage.

Nairn, T. (2000) *After Britain.* London: Granta Books.

Nelson, D. D. (1998) *National Manhood. Capitalist Citizenship and the Imagined Fraternity of White Men.* Durham: Duke University Press.

Neumann, F. L. (1942) *Behemoth: The Structure and Practice of National Socialism.* London: Victor Gollancz.

O'Hanlon, R. and Washbrook, D. (1992) After orientalism: culture, criticism, and politics in the third world, *Comparative Studies in Society and History*, 34(1): 141–67.

O'Neill, W. L. (1971) *Coming Apart: An Informal History of America in the 1960s*. Chicago, IL: Quadrangle Books.

Parkin, F. (1979) *Marxism and Class Theory. A Bourgeois Critique*. London: Tavistock.

Parsons, T. (1937) *The Structure of Social Action*. New York, NY: McGraw-Hill.

Parsons, T. (1999) Religion in postindustrial America, in B. S. Turner (ed.) *The Talcott Parsons Reader*, pp. 300–20. Oxford: Blackwell.

Perl, J. M (1989) *Skepticism and Modern Enmity. Before and After Eliot*. Baltimore, MD: Johns Hopkins Press.

Peterson, P. (1999) Gray dawn: the global aging crisis, *Foreign Affairs*, 78(1): 42–55.

Phillipson, C. (1998) *Reconstructing Old Age: New Agendas in Social Theory and Practice*. London and New Delhi: Sage Publications.

Pilcher, J. (1994) Mannheim's sociology of generations: an undervalued legacy, *American Journal of Sociology*, 45(3): 481–95.

Pilcher, J. (1995) *Age and Generation in Modern Britain*. Oxford: Oxford University Press.

Podhoretz, N. (1967) *Breaking Ranks: A Political Memoir*. London: Weidenfeld and Nicolson.

Popper, K. ([1945] 1995) *The Open Society and Its Enemies*. London: Routledge.

Pratt, R. (1990) *Rhythm and Resistance: Explorations in the Political Uses of Popular Music*. New York: Praeger.

Putnam, D. (1993) *Making Democracy Work. Civic Traditions in Modern Italy*. Princeton, NJ: Princeton University Press.

Putnam, R. D. (2000) *Bowling Alone: The Collapse and Revival of American Community*. New York, NY and London: Simon and Schuster.

Rawls, J. (1971) *A Theory of Justice*. Cambridge, MA: Harvard University Press.

Reich, C. A. (1970) *The Greening of America*. Harmondsworth: Penguin Books.

Reich, R. (1991) *The Work of Nations. Preparing Ourselves for 21st Century Capitalism*. New York, NY: Random House.

Riggs, A. and Turner, B. S. (2000) Pie-eyed optimists: baby-boomers the optimistic generation?, *Social Indicators Research*, 52: 73–93.

Righart, H. (1995) *De Eindeloze Jaren Zestig: Geschiedenis van een Generatie-Conflict (Endless Sixties: History of a Generation Conflict)*. Amsterdam: De Arbeiderspers.

Riley, M. W. (1987) On the significance of age in sociology, *American Sociological Review*, 52(1): 1–14.

Riley, M. W., Foner, A. and Waring, J. (1988) Sociology of age, in N. Smelser (ed.) *Handbook of Sociology*, pp. 243–90. Newbury Park: Sage.

Rodgers, C. (1998) The influence of *The Second Sex* on the French feminist scene, in R. Evans (ed.) *Simone de Beauvoir's* The Second Sex: *New Interdisciplinary Essays*, pp. 59–96. Manchester: Manchester University Press.

Rojek, C. (2001) Stuart Hall, in A. Elliott and B. S. Turner (eds) *Profiles in Contemporary Social Theory*, pp. 360–70. London: Sage.

Rojek, C. and Turner, B. S. (eds) (1993) *Forget Baudrillard?* London and New York, NY: Routledge.

Rojek, C. and Turner, B. S. (eds) (1998) *The Politics of Jean-Francois Lyotard: Justice and Political Theory*. London: Routledge.

Rorty, R. (1989) *Contingency, Irony and Solidarity*. Cambridge: Cambridge University Press.

Rorty, R. (1998) *Achieving Our Country: Leftist Thought in Twentieth-century America*. Cambridge, MA: Harvard University Press.

Roseneil, S. (1995) *Disarming Patriarchy*. Buckingham: Open University Press.

Rowbotham, S. (1990) *The Past Is Before Us: Feminism in Action Since the 1960s*. Harmondsworth: Penguin.

Rushdie, S. (1988) *The Satanic Verses*. London: Viking.

Ryder, N. (1964) Notes on the concept of population, *American Journal of Sociology*, 69: 447–63.

Ryder, N. (1965) The cohort as a concept in the study of social change, *American Sociological Review*, 30: 843–61.

Said, E. W. (1978) *Orientalism*. Harmondsworth: Penguin Books.

Said, E. W. ([1979] 1992) *The Question of Palestine*. London: Vintage.

Said, E. W. (1981) *Covering Islam: How the Media and Experts Determine How We See The World*. London, Melbourne and Henley: Routledge and Kegan Paul.

Said, E. W. (1994) *Culture and Imperialism*. London: Vintage.

Said, E. W. (1999) *Out of Place: A Memoir*. London: Granta Books.

Sartre, J.-P. (1948) *The Anti-Semite and Jew*. New York, NY: Schocken Books.

Sartre, J.-P. (1999) *War Diaries: Notebooks From a Phoney War 1939–40*, trans. Q. Hoare. London: Verso Classics.

Sawicki, J. (1991) *Disciplining Foucault: Feminism, Power and the Body*. New York, NY and London: Routledge.

Saxton, A. (1990) *The Rise and Fall of the White Republic: Class Politics and Mass Culture in Nineteenth-Century America*. London: Verso.

Schelsky, H. (1963) *Die Skeptische Generation. Eine Soziologie der Deutschen Jugend*. Dusseldorf: Diederichs.

Schneider, B. (1988) Political generations and the contemporary women's movement, *Sociological Inquiry*, 58: 4–21.

Schwartz, B. (1982) The social context of commemoration: a study in collective memory, *Social Forces*, 61(2): 374–97.

Scott, J. (2000) Is it a different world to when you were growing up? Generational effects on social representations and child-rearing values, *British Journal of Sociology*, 51(2): 355–76.

Scriven, M. (1999) *Jean-Paul Sartre: Politics and Culture in Post-war France*. Basingstoke: Macmillan.

Sennett, R. (1998) *The Corrosion of Character. The Personal Consequences of Work in the New Capitalism.* New York, NY: W. W. Norton.

Sheridan, A. (1986) *Michel Foucault: The Will to Live.* London and New York, NY: Tavistock Publications.

Sikora, R. I. and Barry, B. (eds) (1978) *Obligations to Future Generations.* Philadelphia, PA: Temple University Press.

Silesky, B. (1990) *Ferlinghetti: The Artist in his Time.* New York, NY: Warner Books.

Skelton, R. (ed.) (1964) *Poetry of the Thirties.* Harmondsworth: Penguin.

Smart, B. (1998) Postmodern social theory, in B. S. Turner (ed.) *The Blackwell Companion to Social Theory,* pp. 396–428. Oxford: Blackwell Publishers.

Smith, C. (2000) *Christian America? What Evangelicals Really Want.* Berkeley, CA: University of California Press.

Stearns, H. (1921) *America and the Young Intellectual.* New York, NY: George H. Doran.

Stratton, J. and Ang, I. (1996) On the impossibility of a global cultural studies. 'British' cultural studies in an 'international' frame, in D. Morley and K.-H. Chen (eds) *Stuart Hall: Critical Dialogues in Cultural Studies,* pp. 361–91. London and New York, NY: Routledge.

Stoekl, A. (1992) *Agonies of the Intellectual: Commitment, Subjectivity and the Performative in the Twentieth-Century French Tradition.* Lincoln, NE and London: University of Nebraska Press.

Swerdlow, A. (1993) *Women Strike for Peace: Traditional Motherhood and Radical Politics in the 1960s.* Chicago, IL and London: Chicago University Press.

Takaki, R. (1990) *Iron Cages: Race and Culture in Nineteenth-Century America.* Oxford: Oxford University Press.

Talmon, J. L. (1952) *The Origins of Totalitarian Democracy.* Harmondsworth: Penguin.

Therborn, G. (1998) Critical theory and the legacy of twentieth-century Marxism, in B. S. Turner (ed.) *The Blackwell Companion to Social Theory.* Oxford: Blackwell Publishers.

Theweleit, K. (1987) *Male Fantasies* (2 volumes). Cambridge: Polity Press.

Tocqueville, A. de (1945) *Democracy in America.* New York, NY: Vintage.

Touraine, A. (2000) *Can We Live Together? Equality and Difference.* Cambridge and Oxford: Polity Press.

Turner, B. (1991) *Religion and Social Theory.* London: Sage.

Turner, B. S. (1998) Introduction, in B. S. Turner (ed.) *The Blackwell Companion to Social Theory.* Oxford: Blackwell.

Turner, B. S. (1999) *Classical Sociology.* London, Thousand Oaks, CA, New Delhi: Sage Publications.

Turner, B. S. (2000a) Edward Said and the exilic ethic on being out of place, *Theory, Culture and Society,* 17(6): 125–9.

Turner, B. S. (2000b) Cosmopolitan virtue: loyalty and the city, in E. Isin (ed.) *Democracy, Citizenship and the Global City,* pp. 129–47. London: Routledge.

Vincent, John A. (1999) *Politics, Power and Old Age*. Buckingham, Philadelphia, PA: Open University Press.

Von Hayek, F. A. ([1944] 1980) *The Road to Serfdom*. Chicago, IL: University of Chicago Press.

Walby, S. (1992) Woman and nation, *International Journal of Comparative Sociology*, 33(1–2): 81–100.

Wald, A. M. (1987) *The New York Intellectuals: The Rise and Decline of the Anti-Stalinist Left from the 1930s to the 1980s*. Chapel Hill, NC: University of North Carolina Press.

Walder, D. (ed.) (1990) *Literature in the Modern World: Critical Essays and Documents*. Oxford: Oxford University Press in association with The Open University.

Walker, A. (ed.) (1996) *The New Generational Contract: Intergenerational Relations, Old Age and Welfare*. London: UCL Press.

Wallace, C. (1997) *Greer: Untamed Shrew*. Melbourne: Macmillan.

Walzer, M. (1986) Interpretation and Social Criticism. Cambridge, MA: Harvard University Press.

Ward, B. (1998) *Just My Soul Responding: Rhythm and Blues, Black Consciousness and Race Relations*. London: UCL Press.

Waters, M. (1996) *Daniel Bell*. London: Routledge.

Wattenberg, E. (1986) Fate of the baby boomers and their children, *Social Work*, 31 (January/February): 20–8.

Watts, M. (1975) The call and response of popular music: the impact of American pop music in Europe, in C. W. E. Bigsby (ed.) *Superculture: American Popular Culture and Europe*, pp. 123–39. London: Paul Elek.

Werbner, P. (1991) Introduction II: Black and ethnic leaderships in Britain: A theoretical overview, in P. Werbner and M. Anwar (eds) *Black and Ethnic Leaderships: The Cultural Dimensions of Political Action*, pp. 15–40. London and New York, NY: Routledge.

Weyman, A. (1995) Modernization, generations and the economy of life-time. Unpublished conference paper by the American Sociological Association (ASA).

Whalen, J. and Flacks, R. (1989) *Beyond the Barricades*. Philadelphia, PA: Temple University Press.

Williams, R. (1958) *Culture and Society 1780–1950*. London: Chatto and Windus.

Williams, R. (1989) *What I Came to Say*. London: Hutchinson.

Wilson, E. (1952) *The Shores of Light. A Literary Chronicle of the Twenties and Thirties*. New York, NY: Vintage.

Wohl, R. (1979) *The Generation of 1914*. Cambridge: Cambridge University Press.

Woolf, V. ([1938] 1977) *The Three Guineas*. London: Hogarth Press.

Woolf, V. ([1938] 1991) *Three Guineas*. London: Hogarth Press.

Wyatt, D. (1993) *Out of the Sixties. Storytelling and the Vietnam Generation*. Cambridge: Cambridge University Press.

Yuval-Davis, N. and Anthias, F. (1989) *Woman–Nation–State*. Houndsmills, Basingstoke and London: Macmillan Press.

Zamyatin, Y. ([1934] 1993) *We*, trans. S. C. Brown. London: Penguin.

Index

RISK

Roy Boyne

- What is risk?
- Who defines the risks we worry about?
- How do risks divide our society?

The term 'risk' occurs throughout contemporary social analysis and political commentary. It is now virtually a legal requirement that large organizations throughout the world establish formal risk assessment and risk management procedures. Increasingly dense communication and media networks alert huge numbers of people and organizations to a widening range of threats and possibilities. A basic understanding of the risks themselves may require specific technical knowledge, of basic chemistry, or the psychology of motivation, or of contrasting interpretations of injustices deep within the past. However, at the same time as attending to specific risks, there are general questions which need answering.

This wide-ranging and concisely written text is devoted to these general questions, exploring issues such as the measurement of risk in its social context, the idea that the mass media or the political opposition always exaggerate risk, and the notion that the advice of the expert is the best we can get as far as risks are concerned. It asks if there are more risks now and whether a certain level of risk is inevitable or even desirable, and considers for example whether interference with nature has led us to a world which is just too full of risks. Each chapter in the book addresses a basic element of risk, and in all, this represents an essential text for students of social theory and the wider social sciences.

Contents
Acknowledgements – The limits of calculation – Risk in the media – Cultural variation or cultural rapture? – Risk-taking – Expert cultures – Risk society? – References – Index.

c.160pp   0 335 20829 0 (pbk)   0 335 20830 4 (hbk)

GENDER AND SOCIAL THEORY

Mary Evans

- What is the most significant aspect of current literature on gender?
- How does this literature engage with social theory?
- How does the recognition of gender shift the central arguments of social theory?

We know that gender defines and shapes our lives. The question addressed by *Gender and Social Theory* is that of exactly how this process occurs, and what the social consequences, and the consequences for social theory, might be. The emergence of feminist theory has enriched our understanding of the impact of gender on our individual lives and the contemporary social sciences all recognize gender differentiation in the social world. The issue, however, which this book discusses is the more complex question of the extent to which social theory is significantly disrupted, disturbed or devalued by the fuller recognition of gender difference. We know that gender matters, but Mary Evans examines whether social theory is as blind to gender as is sometimes argued and considers the extent to which a greater awareness of gender truly shifts the concerns and conclusions of social theory. Written by an author with an international reputation, this is an invaluable text for students and an essential reference in the field.

Contents
Series foreword – Acknowledgement – Introduction – Enter women – The meaning of work – The world of intimacy – The gendered self – The real world – Now you see it, now you don't – Notes – Bibliography – Index.

c.160pp   0 335 20864 9 (pbk)   0 335 20865 7 (hbk)

ECONOMY, CULTURE AND SOCIETY

Barry Smart

> . . . excellent . . . a probing survey of classic and contemporary social theory . . . extremely well written and organized . . . one of the best overviews of contemporary economy, culture and society I have read.
>
> Professor Douglas Kellner, UCLA

> . . . an authoritative analysis and a definitive defence of sociology as a critical theory of the market, politics and social institutions. A balanced and thorough critique of the neo-liberal revolution.
>
> Professor Bryan Turner, University of Cambridge

- How have economic processes and transformations been addressed within classical and contemporary social thought?
- What impact have the market system and market forces had on social life?
- How has the imbalance between the public and private sectors been felt in contemporary society?

Economic factors and processes are at the heart of contemporary social and cultural life and this book is designed to refocus social theorizing to reflect that fact. The author re-interprets the work of classical theorists and, in the context of the move towards social regulation and protection in the 19th and early 20th centuries, he discusses more recent transformations in capitalist economic life that have led to greater flexibility, forms of disorganization, and a neo-liberal regeneration of the market economy. As our lives have become subject to a process of commodification, market forces have assumed an increasing prominence, and the imbalance in resources between private and public sectors has been aggravated. This illuminating text addresses these central concerns, drawing on the work of key social and economic thinkers.

Contents

c.192pp   0 335 20910 6 (pbk)   0 335 20911 4 (hbk)

MAKING SENSE OF SOCIAL MOVEMENTS

Nick Crossley

effectively demonstrates the enduring importance of 'classical' social movement theory . . . and provides a cutting edge critical review of recent theoretical developments. This is one of the most important general theoretical texts on social movements for some years.

Paul Bagguley, University of Leeds

- Why and how do social movements emerge?
- In which ways are social movements analysed?
- Can our understanding be enhanced by new perspectives?

Making Sense of Social Movements offers a clear and comprehensive overview of the key sociological approaches to the study of social movements. The author argues that each of these approaches makes an important contribution to our understanding of social movements but that none is adequate on its own. In response he argues for a new approach which draws together key insights within the solid foundations of Pierre Bourdieu's social theory of practice. This new approach transcends the barriers which still often divide European and North American perspectives of social movements, and also those which divide recent approaches from the older 'collective behaviour' approach. The result is a theoretical framework which is uniquely equipped for the demands of modern social movement analysis. The clear and concise style of the text, as well as its neat summaries of key concepts and approaches, will make this book invaluable for undergraduate courses. It will also be an essential reference for researchers.

Contents

c.192pp   0 335 20602 6 (Paperback)   0 335 20303 4 (Hardback)